THE GOOD
FIGHT

Wanting to Leave,
Choosing to Stay, and the
Powerful Practice for
Loving Faithfully

THE GOOD FIGHT

JANA KRAMER AND MICHAEL CAUSSIN

HarperOne
An Imprint of HarperCollins*Publishers*

HarperOne

FIRST EDITION

Designed by Leah Carlson-Stanisic

Library of Congress Cataloging-in-Publication Data

Names: Kramer, Jana, 1983– author. | Caussin, Michael, 1987– author.
Title: The good fight / Jana Kramer and Michael Caussin.
Description: First edition. | New York, NY : HarperOne, 2020
Identifiers: LCCN 2020010109 (print) | LCCN 2020010110 (ebook) | ISBN 9780062964236 (hardcover) | ISBN 9780062964243 (trade paperback) | ISBN 9780062964267 (ebook)
Subjects: LCSH: Marital conflict. | Interpersonal relations—Psychological aspects. | Forgiveness.
Classification: LCC HQ734 .K73 2020 (print) | LCC HQ734 (ebook) | DDC 306.872—dc23
LC record available at https://lccn.loc.gov/2020010109
LC ebook record available at https://lccn.loc.gov/2020010110

20 21 22 23 24   LSC   10 9 8 7 6 5 4 3

To my wife:

Our journey hasn't been what I promised you, and for that I am eternally sorry. That being said, there is so much I wouldn't change about it. I wouldn't be even half the man I am today if it wasn't for you, and the only reason I am is because you stayed. You chose to fight this Good Fight with me. You chose me, you chose our children, and through all of this you even chose yourself. I am captivated by your beauty, fascinated by your strength, mesmerized by your personality, and motivated by your moxie. You are the one for me and I am certain about that. God has put us together for reasons and I have the utmost faith that it was for all the right ones. Thank you for being you, for choosing me, and for always reminding me that I am enough.

I love you with all my heart and I am forever yours,

Michael

To my husband:

I wouldn't change one page of our story. There is so much beauty in the struggles and in the hard times, and though it was hard to see that then, I see it now, as I love you more today than yesterday. Thank you thank you for fighting so hard not only for me, but for yourself and for our two babies. We would not be here today if it wasn't for the amount of work, patience, recovery, empathy, and love you have given this relationship. I respect the hell out of you, Mike. I love you.

xo,

Jana

To our Jolie and Jace:

Our strength on this journey derived from our unconditional love for you. Our shared motivation was to give you the family you both deserve under one roof. You two deserve a house full of love, of fun, of patience, of understanding, of forgiveness, and of grace. Every day you remind us of why we fought and why we keep fighting for our marriage and for our family. You two are truly gifts from God and we are forever thankful to have such beautiful blessings in our life.

Love,

Mom and Dad

Contents

What Will We Ever Fight About?

Mike

It was early evening exactly a year ago. Our family had just finished dinner. Jolie, our "threenager," was crying, battling a bath. Jana was trying to negotiate with promises of ice cream. Jace, our newborn, was fussy because it was bottle time. All this while I tried to make a dent in the dishes before taking over with Jolie so Jana could get Jace his bottle. Two crying kids, a dirty kitchen, two dogs running between our legs, begging for scraps—after a full day working so we could afford all this madness.

And oh yeah, there in the back of my mind, marinating, was the argument that Jana and I had had earlier in the day that had set the two of us off balance—and, frankly, at odds—all evening.

My hands plunged in dishwater, I replayed the argument and the aftermath in my mind, and this is where my thoughts went: *I'm definitely in the right. But I overreacted when Jana criticized me. I can see her side, and I wish she knew that. But if I give in now, if I say I'm sorry, she'll feel like she can pick fights about every little thing, and I'll end up being a pushover. She's already giving me the silent treatment. Maybe I shouldn't say anything and see whether she'll come to me. I wish we could just move past this.*

Why do we need to have another fight?

Thinking back on that night, I want to puke. Seriously, I feel sick writing that. So much anxiety fueled by my pride, guilt, loneliness, and uncertainty. So much uncertainty. Would our marriage survive another fight? Why are we fighting about this stupid shit? Does every couple fight like this?

This scene probably sounds familiar to you. Maybe you have kids, too, and life is in a permanent state of *Groundhog Day*–esque chaos. Or maybe it's just you and your partner. Or maybe you're single but know you have some work to do in relationships before you jump back in the game. Regardless, if you've ever felt the way I felt that evening doing dishes while a stupid fight from earlier in the day hung over your house and family and relationship and mental state like the heaviest blanket in the world, you're not alone.

As I finished the dishes I wondered which direction this night was headed. Would we (1) do the knock-down drag-out screaming and crying thing? or (2) avoid each other? or (3) have a weird passive-aggressive conversation that would "resolve" things but still leave me wondering whether we would fight again tomorrow?

And that's when it happened. I looked up. Jana looked up. She mouthed "I love you" to me, and I mouthed "I love you" back to her. And I could see that she meant it, and I knew in my heart that I love this woman and want the best for her and us and this incredible family we have created. That moment doing dishes was a turning point.

I'd been asking myself that question: *Why do we need to have another fight?* But now I realize I should have been asking, *Why do we need to fight the way we've always fought?*—that is, the way we'd always been fighting: talking over each other, holding grudges, bringing up old shit, name-calling, and door-slamming. It occurred to me that we don't actually need to do any of those things ever again. I wondered whether we could both completely and forever just *stop*.

I know what you're thinking: this sounds too good to be true. And it was. It's not like we got into bed that night, clinked our wineglasses, and watched the most recent episode of *Ozark* without addressing our previous argument. We still didn't handle it perfectly, but we handled it better. Ultimately, that's all we wanted to do. We decided that even if we were destined to fight every day for the rest of our lives, we would resolve to at least try to do it better.

And that's when everything changed.

Love Story

In case you don't know already, our love story hasn't been a fairy tale, even though it started off that way. Let me set the scene for you.

It's a beautiful spring afternoon in 2015. The sun is beginning its descent, with shades of pink and orange and red glowing onto the rolling hills outside of Charlottesville, Virginia. The landscape is radiant with the greens and browns of the surrounding vineyards. One hundred people take their seats. I walk down the aisle, then Jana does. Vows are shared, drinks are consumed, congratulations are passed around, dancing begins, and then in the blink of an eye the night is done. The party is over and everyone heads their separate ways. Our whirlwind romance of the previous eleven months has hit its storybook climax.

Jana and I said "I love you" after ten days of knowing each other. We moved in together after three months, bought a house after four months. We were engaged at six and married at eleven. Oh yeah, and expecting our first kid at the one-year mark. That may come as a shock to you (it did for everyone else in our lives), but none of this seemed surprising to *us*. It was a love like we never imagined; it was the real deal.

I remember one morning early on, we were lying in my bedroom at my Baltimore house. (I had just brought Jana in town to meet my family of friends, because let's be honest, your friends' approval is the most important, right?) The sun was just beginning to come through the blinds as we gradually awoke from our Fourth of July hangovers. It was the first time we had spent the night together, but it felt like the five hundredth. We were teasing each other, and I jokingly said that I hoped we wouldn't be one of those couples who fight all the time.

In that moment—I shit you not—we both smiled, looked into each other's eyes, and actually said to one another at the same time, *"But what will we ever fight about?"*

Little did we know that just six weeks later in that very same bedroom in Baltimore we would wake up with a completely different feeling. That was the moment that our storybook fairy tale got kicked in the face by reality. I had cheated on Jana, and she woke up that morning to learn about it in the form of a direct message on social media. I had that punch-in-the-gut feeling where I knew what was happening before she even said it. I could see it on her face and feel it in the air.

Then, in July 2016, I admitted to having multiple affairs. Jana gave me an ultimatum: either go somewhere to figure out what the hell was wrong with me, or she was done. So I chose the former, and after plenty of therapy and counseling, I realized that at least part of my behavior was due to an addiction that I never knew I had—and that I have been working on ever since.

Suddenly, as if out of nowhere, that question "What will we ever fight about?" seemed like a joke. We had a lifetime supply of material now.

Jana

No one gets married because they think it's going to be hell. I guess the question I ask myself now is, *Did I really expect it to be a fairy tale?*

I think I did expect perfection. And maybe you did, too. It's not naive or silly to think those thoughts because who wouldn't want a fairy-tale marriage or relationship of constant bliss and love? However, it's also okay to be bummed about the state of your marriage or relationship if it's not what you imagined. Plenty of times Mike and I have sat down and talked about how it's a lot harder than we thought, or sometimes it's just not what we had pictured. And you know what? That's okay. It's what you do next that will define the rest of your story. Which is why I'm so glad Mike and I have gone through hell to learn these things under the worst circumstances, so maybe you and your partner don't have to.

A Modern Fairy Tale

So why did I want a *fairy-tale* marriage? Maybe it was from the thousand times as a kid I pressed the "play" button on *Cinderella* or swooned over Prince Eric from *The Little Mermaid*. I was raised on princes and happily-ever-afters. You might have thought that fairy-tale concept would have been squashed in my brain from all the times I saw my mom and dad fight, but it wasn't. It only propelled me more into wanting that fairy tale. My relationship history was a mix of fleeing at the first sign of trouble and playing the "happy princess" even when the relationship wasn't healthy or I knew it wasn't right. After years of that, I realized it was time to try something different. It wasn't until this relationship with Mike that I stayed after it got tough. Now I've coined our marriage as the "modern fairy tale."

A modern fairy tale is our version of a love story, and I would argue that every *true* love story isn't a fairy tale but a *modern* fairy tale. No relationship is perfect. It's just not. But that doesn't mean it's doomed. It just means that you're human, and humans are complex creatures. Lots of marriage vows say that you'll stay together "in sickness and in health" and "in good times and in bad."

To our knowledge, they never say you'll stay together only if "we never disagree or fight."

Speaking of fighting . . . I'm sure you can think of one couple you know that seems to have the "perfect relationship." Yes, go ahead and picture them in your mind. I'm going to guess this is a couple that you've never witnessed having a fight, or when everyone else is complaining about their significant other at girls' night, this person stays suspiciously quiet on the matter and you think, "Wow, is it possible to have zero disagreements with your partner?"

Comparing marriages and relationships is the worst thing you can do for your sanity—and for your relationship. Problem is, though, we all do it. It's easy when Sally and Joe seem so in love, always kissing, always laughing, and never talking about their fights. And sure, maybe Sally and Joe do have a near-perfect relationship, but we also don't know what they did to get there.

On the other hand, we have all most likely experienced those couples who fight all the time. You know the ones: you're out with a group of friends and they start going at it and everyone rolls their eyes, thinking, "There go Al and Christine again." When you're around this kind of couple, you may look at your relationship and start to feel pretty good about yourselves. You start thinking, "Hey, we're doing pretty good; I mean, at least we aren't like Al and Christine." But that can be just as detrimental as comparing your relationship to a "perfect" one. Relationships are extremely subjective. Everything depends on what works for you and what works for your partner—and then figuring out how to work together.

As you read this book, I encourage you to not compare your relationship to my and Mike's relationship. You might read some of our arguments and think, *Whoa, they're a mess!*—or better yet, *a hot mess*. Or you might read a particularly awesome moment for us and feel like shit about your love life—and then the next thing you know, you're picking a fight with your loved one because of it. The point is that comparing isn't fun, and in the long run it's not going to make you feel better or your relationship any stronger. Trust me on this, though I've done it so many times and I've also sadly thrown it in Mike's face and compared him to other men and said a time or two, "Hey why can't you be like Nick or talk to me like Kristen's husband?" This not only causes a fight but a large amount of shame for Mike, and at the end of the day, that's not nice or fair. There are healthier ways to communicate (see Chapter 4), and you better believe there are ways to improve so you're not caught on the hot mess train we've been on a time or ten.

I never thought Mike and I would be fighting types. As he said earlier, we both wondered, *What will we ever fight about?* When I first met him, it was one of those moments that if I had heard anyone describe falling in love in this way, I would have rolled my eyes. Simply put (and get ready to roll your eyes), he made my heart skip a beat. Yup, I said it. It was a whirlwind interaction, from following him back on Twitter to an impromptu "Hey I have a show in Chicago in a few days, you should come" to his opening the door of my tour bus. I was in the back of the bus, and when I saw him walking in, I not only had to catch my breath, but I thought, *Wow, this is it.*

That little girl watching *Cinderella* over and over might have believed in the "feeling" you would have when you met "the one," but as cynical as I had become, I no longer believed there was such a thing until that perfect day in Chicago in June. Michael instantly made me feel accepted and not crazy for my past—all on that first day I met him. He was familiar in a way that made me feel safe and protected. I knew I was in it for the long haul.

What Is The Good Fight?

First, a disclaimer. We've been through a lot of therapy. The system and principles we talk about and what has helped us aren't set in stone and don't necessarily apply to everyone. We aren't experts, but after years and years of trial and error, we've come to understand what works *for us*.

When we refer to "The Good Fight," we're not talking about one standalone argument or little disagreements; we're talking about the idea of reimagining your relationship as something you don't fight *against* but fight *for*.

Let's pause here for a moment. It may seem obvious, but when the weight of bills, chores, kids, and jobs starts pitting you and your partner against each other, it's pretty easy to forget why you're in this thing to begin with. However, when you make this change in mindset—thinking of your marriage as The Good Fight, as something you fight *for*—you instinctively change the way you interact with your partner.

When you get married, you make a commitment, and you can think of The Good Fight as a recommitment . . . to your relationship, your family, and your best life yet. We hope that through reading this book you can get to the place where you have a greater love and appreciation for your partner in those inevitable difficult moments because you realize that that person is willing to fight through life with you no matter what. What a powerful and loving concept! That human being whom you are sharing your life with has chosen to fight for that love with you every day. That person may have different opinions, morals, interests, or even beliefs than you have. Yet he or she is still choosing to battle each day with you and for you.

That's *The Good Fight*.

Each chapter of this book explores a principle for fighting The Good Fight with your loved one, from "claiming your baggage" to "trusting the process." But fighting The Good Fight also means still having the inevitable disagreement, *and* having the inevitable major relationship crisis. What's the biggest threat to The Good Fight? It's those little arguments you have with your partner that you never seem to work through. That's why we open each chapter with an argument we've had in our past—to help you realize YOU ARE NOT ALONE and to see the ways sometimes single arguments are your best chance to practice loving each other: listening, being present, working on yourself, and quieting the urge to bring up old shit, name-call, or be defensive. Some of these arguments are straight-up embarrassing for us to relate, but if we've learned anything from our *Whine Down with Jana Kramer and Michael Caussin* podcast, it's that being open and honest about fights is the best way to be able to do it better the next time around.

Fighting = Loving

You may be wondering how focusing on fighting can help grow your relationship, and you may even be scratching your head at the thought that fighting is the key to that connection, transparency, and loving joy you desperately want. We get it; it's an unusual concept. Many books explore the ways to *prevent* fighting. But let's cut the crap: we all know fighting is inevitable, and we'll fight with our partners fairly regularly, regardless of whether our relationship is feeling fantastic or not.

We're just embracing the concept that you can learn about your partner and grow closer through those inevitable disagreements. The worst thing you can do is head into those fights ill-equipped to fight fair and show respect, listen, and communicate. When you do that, you compromise the entire Good Fight of your journey together by bringing your worst self to the most meaningful moments. Fights can be revealing, a lens into your partner's needs and communication style. They can show the way your partner is changing or evolving as a person, and give you a chance to express yourself and be heard and challenged.

So, yes, WE WANT YOU TO FIGHT! If you opened this book to learn how to stop fighting, well, this book isn't for you. The truth is, you *will* fight, and we encourage you not to run away from that. Sometimes you need to fight *even more* than you are right now. But the fights don't have to move you apart, and in fact, they can move you one thousand times closer together. We promise.

We get that this all sounds easier said than done, and it is. Like anything worthwhile, The Good Fight takes time, practice, and patience. But the chapters of this book will help you navigate through arguments in healthy ways and learn about yourself and your partner. Learning each other's needs, wants, and expectations and learning how you both receive love are all vital to creating the kind of home environment you deserve.

We learned all the things we cover in this book the hard way. We didn't have the necessary discussions around a lot of these topics because we didn't know how. It was a classic example of "you don't know what you don't know." But without these past years of fighting, discovering each other, and introspective learning, we wouldn't be where we are today.

The Good Fight is more than dealing with arguments, fights, and disagreements. It's about fighting for the life you want, fighting for the relationship you want—but you just don't know how to get there.

Important Questions

When it comes to conflict in a relationship, there are stereotypes that can skew your beliefs about your own relationship or relationships in general. It's easy to envy the couples who claim, "We never fight, he/she is so amazing"—blah blah. Or the ones who look picture perfect on Instagram or Facebook and seem to have it all figured out, judging from the pictures they post. We've all thought, "I wish I had what they have" or "If I had that I would be happy." Wrong! The opposite stereotype would be the couples who never stop fighting and constantly bitch about or blame each other. These days, people hit the "eject" button and leave relationships at the first sign of confrontation. So it seems there is no in between; it's either "perfection" or "disaster."

Our intention is to reassure you that there *is* a middle ground. Your relationship doesn't have to follow those stereotypes or "rules." If things are going south, it doesn't mean that y'all aren't meant to be together. By using the tools we talk about throughout this book, you can make a positive difference in your relationship.

Again, we are NOT experts, nor do we claim to be, but we've been to hell and back; if we can find the light at the end of the tunnel, so can you. We want to help you move your relationship in the direction that you want it to go and also help you answer some questions that might come up along the way:

- Why am I not happy?

- How do I get my partner to listen to my feelings?

- Is this worth fighting for?

- Any time I bring up an issue with my partner, he/she gets defensive; what can I do?

- How do I remain hopeful during the tough times?

- How do I fight through the emotional triggers?

- What do I do if I'm the only one fighting?

In the end, it's most important to work on yourself. Your relationship will benefit the most and you will maximize your happiness if you focus on what *you* can do differently and not on what you think your partner needs to do differently. You'll not only learn much more about your partner, but you'll also better understand your interworkings as a couple.

We hope you learn to love The Good Fight within your relationship. We're optimistic that if you learn to put down your swords and shields and lean into one another, the silver lining you'll discover around the moments of pain and darkness will be worth it.

Is It Still Worth Fighting For?

Why is your marriage or relationship not the fairy tale you imagined? What went wrong? Do you communicate badly? Have you drifted apart? These are questions that you need to answer for yourself, but we hope that reading this book will help you modernize your fairy tale to make it the best marriage/relationship it can be.

After you nail down the reasons why your relationship isn't what you imagined, next comes the question, "How did things get this way?" and more important, "How do I know it's worth it?" Given our relationship history, people ask us that question constantly. "How do you know if it's still worth fighting for?" The answer we've discovered through our years of healing and growing is this: if both people are willing to fight for the relationship, then there's enough fuel to keep going.

We can understand and empathize with wanting to stay in a relationship no matter what, but it's very hard to grow in a marriage when only one person is doing the work. We never would have lasted and gotten stronger if only one of us was doing the work. It's imperative that both of you are fighting for the same thing: for love, for growth, for understanding, and for the ability to heal *together*. It would be a very hard and lonely road to fight The Good Fight alone, so we hope that with the tools in the chapters to come, you and your partner can start to truly fight this *together*.

1 Claim Your Baggage

Jana

We were packing for yet another *Whine Down* podcast tour, and our room was a mess. The suitcases were on the bed and clothes thrown everywhere. Mike and I were frantically packing with two kids asking for our attention at the same time. As my bag started to overfill, I noticed three-quarters of Mike's bag was still empty. (Just a small sidebar here: my bag is the smallest of the bags, while Mike has a very large one, which he defends because he's bigger.) So I threw in my makeup bag and one sweater to fill the hole and then threw my laptop in his backpack. I mean, I would have done the same for him if he had needed extra space.

I guess I should have anticipated the eye roll and deep, loud sigh when he opened his bag and saw my stuff in there. It's not the first time I've heard that sigh and felt his annoyance when I do that. You might wonder, Well, why not just get a bigger bag? To which I say, Very valid question, but I don't like to check bags. My question has always been, Why can't he carry my extra stuff?

Mike

This is one of those situations that happens often in our relationship because of the amount we travel. But honestly, I still haven't come to terms with the fact that Jana relies on me to carry her extra shit. I mean, why is that my responsibility? When traveling, I like to worry about my stuff and that's all. I don't feel the need to be in charge of her stuff as well; we're both adults here. I didn't sign up to carry her stuff . . . or did I?

A lot of you may think that when you enter a new relationship it's a fresh start and you have a clean slate to do it differently this time around. We've both thought the same thing and have even talked about how we wish we could restart our relationship and make all the pain go away. Though it would be great to use a time machine to travel to the beginning of a relationship and do things over, we're all forgetting one important thing.

Most of the reason a relationship goes south isn't because of what your partner did. Sure, he or she might have royally messed up and broken your heart, but the question is, *Why?* Some of you might answer, Well, because he was a manipulative scumbag, or she never stopped nagging. Though again, that might be true, most of the issues that come into play and cause rifts in relationships come from your stuff—your baggage—and how you deal with it. Your baggage isn't easy to identify, and it's even harder to look inside yourself to identify it. But we all need to face it. We all come into a relationship with baggage, and it's on us to know what we're bringing to that relationship.

Some of your baggage might be related to your past, and it's important to be open and honest about your past scars with your partner. If your partner knows about your past and what has shaped you, then he or she can have a front row seat when trying to help in situations or maybe have some insight into why you're reacting the way you are. This insight is how we help "carry" each other's baggage. And boy do Jana and I have a lot . . .

Jana

I remember a night in seventh grade like it was yesterday. I was having a sleepover with one of my best friends, and I heard the front door to our house open and close. This was surprising because it was one o'clock in the morning. I told my friend I would be right back because I was curious to see who the mystery person was coming in so late.

I was hoping it was my brother because what little sister doesn't love to tattle? But as I rounded the corner I was shocked to see it was my dad. When he turned around and saw me, he looked like he had seen a ghost. "Where were you?" I asked him. His response: "Home Depot." It came so fast out of his mouth that I think he truly believed it. I'll tell you who didn't believe it: me. I walked back to my friend with the most confused, sad feeling and told her, "I think my dad is cheating on my mom." My father was the first man to ever lie to me.

It's no surprise I have baggage. But the baggage didn't start accumulating in my twenties—nor, I'm sure, did a lot of yours. I've gone to countless therapists and also attended weekend retreats to get to basically the same conclusion: I started to accumulate my "childhood wounds" around the time I was five years old.

The years after it became clear that my dad was indeed cheating on my mom were consumed with nothing but my parents fighting and my mom trying to make their marriage work. It wasn't until I hit the ninth grade that my mom finally stopped trying and the divorce papers were finalized. My dad started his new family faster than I could blink, and I entered high school wanting men to pay attention to me and tell me that I was "good enough." To this day, that's my biggest struggle—constantly wanting validation from men.

I was craving that "father figure," and boy did I make that obvious; I dated men who were at least fifteen years older than me. The funny thing was that all the men I picked couldn't give me that validating love I was seeking. My first "marriage," when I was nineteen, started after two weeks. (I put "marriage" in scare quotes because my first two—yup, I've been married three times—were marriages in only the technical sense.) Yes, I married him after knowing him only two weeks, and no, I wasn't drunk—although I wish I had been so I would have had a more reasonable excuse for why I did such a childish thing. To make this story even better, we got ourselves a drive-thru wedding in Vegas. Classy AF.

That "marriage" lasted a little over a year. No one knew about it until I had to testify in court that he was my husband. You might wonder why I was doing that. Well, after months of physical abuse, he tried to kill me, and he went to jail for attempted murder. I'll never forget the shame I felt when I told my mom that he had been abusing me for more than a year—and that I had married him. Talk about baggage!

After that, I suffered from massive anxiety attacks and post-traumatic stress disorder. I couldn't drive my car or be in a public place without experiencing debilitating anxiety. I basically moved on to abusing myself through my relationships with men. My "drug" was men and having them fall in love with me. I would date guys, make them say "I love you," and then hightail it out of there and disappear.

In my mid-twenties I met the next guy I married. He was again much older than me, and I slipped right back into trying to prove I was good enough for him to love me. We dated for three years on and off, and we got engaged during the start of my *One Tree Hill* days. Our wedding was beautiful, but there was something about that day that just didn't feel right, so a week later I called it off. I knew in my heart of hearts he wasn't the one. Why didn't I just call off the wedding, you ask? Well, because I'm a people pleaser and I didn't want to ruin anyone's plans, and I thought that just maybe, when I walked down the aisle, my heart would feel something different. But it didn't.

So what does one do after two divorces? Well, I spent my late twenties in therapy offices, at retreats, and nose deep in self-help books. I was determined to change my ways and get healthy. I had a few slips here and there, and I continued to struggle with not feeling I was "good enough," but I started to identify with my childhood wounds and my inner child, and I started to give her a hell of a lot more love.

When I hit thirty I was the best version of myself and truly loved just being by myself, which was something I had never felt very comfortable with. I was confident, in my prime, and genuinely happy. And I met Mike. We shared some very honest talks, and for the first time I wasn't embarrassed about my past. I owned it, and I was in some weird way proud of it—and of me. I told him all my baggage. I told him about my two "marriages." I told him I had major "daddy issues" that made me feel abandoned and like I was never good enough. I also told Mike that I wasn't perfect, that I had cheated in past relationships. To this day I feel bad about having cheated, but with all the work I have done, I can see why I did what I did and how today I am a healthier version of myself.

It was the most honest I had ever been with someone. And I felt free.

Childhood Wounds

Something that needs to be said when talking about baggage and what you bring to a relationship is also the age that you bring to the table—that is, the age when your childhood wounds started. Many times when you're fighting with your partner, the person fighting is that childhood age, not the age of your adult self. Knowing when your partner was "wounded" will give you insight into how he or she will fight—and wouldn't you fight differently if you were fighting with a five-year-old?

When Michael and I started doing therapy, our therapist suggested that he carry a picture of me when I was five years old to remind him that when we fight, that's who he is fighting with. To remind him how differently he would talk to that little girl, how differently he would respond. The only problem with the childhood wounds, though, is that he fights from his ten-year-old self. So you have a ten-year-old and a five-year-old battling it out. Our hope is that we can learn to talk from our adult selves. Unfortunately, one of us always slips back to the child, so the trick is to try to remain your age and bring the child (your partner) back to his or her current age in the present moment. Easier said than done, especially if you're dealing with someone who's acting from the age of a toddler. Lord knows, reasoning with our four-year-old is hard enough, but we give her a lot more love and patience, and that should be the same for your partner.

We haven't discovered a flawless tool that helps us revert back to the age of our adult selves. But we have learned to take space to ground ourselves and ask the question, "How old am I right now?" That helps us to determine whether or not we're in a good space to have a conversation.

The Blame Game

I blamed my dad for a long time, believing that he was the reason I picked bad men because I had seen him yelling at mom and I thought that's what I deserved. Here's what I've learned, though. My mom and dad were just doing the best they could with the wounds they developed when they were children.

I don't fault my parents for the way they raised me or the amount of spaghetti they threw during the epic dinner fights they had. They weren't aware of their wounds, nor did they do healing work until much later in their lives. I can't fault them for what they didn't know, and I also can't fault them for trying to give me the best childhood that they knew how. God knows how much I'll screw Jolie and Jace up, but I know that being aware of how to be a better parent and ultimately healing my childhood wounds will help.

Rebound Time

Rebound time is the time it takes to truly reconnect after a fight or argument. The word "truly" is important here. We spent many times reconnecting after fights thinking everything was okay, when really, one or both of us still had unresolved feelings that we pushed down for the sake of moving on. Well, that doesn't help anyone if those feelings later come out sideways. Truly reconnecting after a fight means that both parties have expressed their feelings and been heard. Simple as that. It is NOT about figuring out who "won" that argument; it IS about both of you feeling understood. We'll dive deeper into "winning" versus "being understood" later in the book to give y'all the steps you need to resolve a fight in such a way that you feel closer to one another afterwards.

Mike

It's difficult to fully understand what events throughout your life shape who you are and *why* you are. It wasn't until I started going to therapy regularly around five years ago that I started to dive more deeply into figuring out the inner workings of me.

Now that I'm a parent I understand that parents do the best that they can, and I know mine did their absolute best. There is no educational program on how to be a parent. You can read all the books or go to all the classes you want, but nothing can prepare you enough for raising a growing human being who is a constantly changing variable in your life. The best education we all receive is the example of our parents, who got it from their parents, who got it from their parents. You get the point.

As a young adult I used to blame my parents for how things had been at times when I was a child. Were they perfect? No, but no parent is. And we can't anticipate how a particular situation will affect our children when they get older. When my parents looked at my report card and saw a B and then asked me why I didn't get an A or what I could do to get an A the next time, they couldn't have anticipated that I would hang on to feelings of not being good enough. They were just trying to push me to be the best that I could be. Or when they criticized me because I didn't brush my teeth—how could they know that I would start lying to them about that to "protect myself"? They couldn't have foreseen lying becoming a constant behavioral trait for me.

Maybe they had a rough day at work or other outside stresses that a ten-year-old doesn't understand, and they were tired of having to remind me to brush my teeth. From one perspective, those could be seen as excuses or rationalizing their behavior or reactions. Now as a parent myself, I see them as just being human. I know that I'm guilty of being a little too harsh with Jolie sometimes. But because of all the work I've done on myself and all the therapy, I can say that I'm more aware of when I'm being that way. So I'm able to stop myself more often or even apologize to Jolie if I know I'm in the wrong.

Everybody has some sort of childhood baggage. We all have our shit. But I love and respect my parents for all that they did for me and my siblings. There was food on the table, a roof over our heads, and they came to damn near every football game I played. We never questioned whether they loved us. Whether verbally or through their actions, they showed that they did. And when Jolie and Jace get older, I can only hope they appreciate me and Jana as much as I appreciate my parents.

My relationship baggage started when I got my heart broken at age sixteen. She went to a neighboring high school, but once school started after a summer of love, I felt like Sandy when Danny Zuko left her high and dry. The summer lovin' was over and I slowly became jaded and more selfish, reconciling this heartbreak by resolving to never let it happen again. So I've dated only a few women in my life. Most of my relationships can be more described as "talking to," which essentially means we were sleeping together but I never committed enough to get my feelings involved. And when I did commit, I inevitably cheated. I couldn't be alone. I absolutely hated being the "bad guy" who cheated, but I couldn't stop. I persuaded myself that when I found "the one," then I would stop. Yeah, that still didn't happen, even when I found her.

Ultimately, I came into my relationship with Jana as an intimacy-avoidant undiagnosed sex addict with anger management issues, who couldn't communicate his feelings and had a constant need for attention while simultaneously needing space. Finish that off with a side of increasing codependent tendencies. That would have been the perfect caption for my speed-dating name tag a few years ago. I mean, can you say winner winner chicken dinner?!

In the past I never would have admitted to any of that. I would have lived in denial, pretending I was the same nice guy everyone saw and loved in all other areas of my life. Now I can own that because I know I'm not alone. I know we all have our baggage. Unfortunately, in my case my baggage severely harmed the woman I love. But I know she's the right one because regardless of knowing my baggage, she still loves me and chooses to be with me. She helps me carry my baggage every day. It's all out there for both of us. We know each other's deepest shit, yet we still choose to stay together, and we still choose to fight The Good Fight. What more could you ask for from your life partner?

Hey Honey, Let Me Help You with Your Baggage

Baggage isn't something we ask for when diving into a new relationship; it's just one of those things that comes with the territory. The question is, are you going to fight it, use it as a weapon, let it come between you? Or are you going to walk over there and help your partner pick that shit up? Are you going to leave room in your suitcase expecting there to be something you have to carry for him? And will you do that willingly? How great would it be for your partner to ask for that space and receive it without any sighs, eye rolls, or comments? Learning your partner's baggage is like reading their diary. You learn some of the most important, most intimate parts about them. You're learning the fundamental reasons why they are who they are—the good, the bad, and the ugly.

We've learned a few helpful tips from our therapists about how to help your partner carry his or her baggage.

1. **REMEMBER WHO IS TALKING TO YOU**: We fight at the age we were when we were wounded. Try to keep this in mind when baggage issues surface.

2. **PRACTICE PATIENCE AND UNDERSTANDING**: Once you remind yourself that a five- or ten-year-old is talking to you, it's a lot easier to be patient and understanding. So remember to be soft and loving.

3. **LISTEN**: Don't focus on solving your partner's problems or trying to make his feelings go away. Instead, focus on listening. That child talking to you wants to be heard and needs to feel safe.

4. **PUT YOURSELF IN YOUR PARTNER'S SHOES**: Imagine how that child is feeling inside right now. That way, it's much easier to remain empathetic.

5. **STAY POSITIVE**: After you make listening your priority, any response, assistance, or guidance needs to remain positive. That inner child doesn't want to feel stupid for

feeling the way she feels, so it's imperative to be optimistic when supporting her.

6. PAY ATTENTION TO PATTERNS: The more we've learned each other's baggage and triggers (see Chapter 3), the more we've been able to stay ahead of certain moments. Sometimes, when that child starts to build up in one of us, the other can anticipate it coming because of past experiences; that person can then validate that inner child by stating they understand and everything is going to be okay.

None of this is easy, by the way. It's difficult to notice those moments when we are in our own world and have our own shit going on. But knowing what to do and what the other person deals with is half the battle. Now we just have to keep practicing so we can become more consistent at being the other's support in those moments. This reminds us of a quotation we once saw that really stayed with us: "Everyone comes with baggage. Find someone who loves you enough to help unpack it."

Last Words

We're leaning into y'all by bringing y'all into our world as we see it. We're sharing our emotional baggage because it has shaped major parts of who we both are. That's exactly what we recommend y'all do in your relationships. That person you want to spend your life with is supposed to be your biggest supporter, your warmest blanket, and your smallest fear. There's no better way to grow into that bond more deeply than by leaning in and sharing your baggage.

Baggage tends to have negative connotations, but it shouldn't. It's an unavoidable thing that we all carry; it's what we choose to do with it that defines how it affects us. Can you rid yourself completely of your emotional baggage? Probably not, but you can use it to strengthen yourself and your relationship. It will always be there, but how much power it has over you is your decision. We've realized that by opening the door to that room full of suitcases, duffle bags, and backpacks and showing each other the contents of each one, we already feel the effect they have on us dissipating. So lean into that person you say those three little words to. Allow that person the opportunity to love you even more deeply.

2 Clean Your Side of the Street

Jana

"We absolutely are NOT hanging that up."

I vividly remember those words coming out of my mouth. It was the day Mike and I moved into our first house back in 2014. It was a beautiful Nashville day, and we were on cloud nine as we opened the door to our new beginning. The radio was blaring Ed Sheeran throughout the house speakers as we started to unbox memories from our past and decorate our future. As I joined Mike in one of the guest rooms, I saw him opening up one of the boxes from his Baltimore house. Out came the most hideous, and I mean absolutely hideous, painting of an Arizona sunset. I love a good sunset, but I thought for sure it was a white elephant gift that he probably got stuck with a few Christmases ago.

I've said that I have no filter, and out came, "We absolutely are NOT hanging that up. Seriously, Michael, that is so damn ugly." Mike was deflated and tried to persuade me that he had spent a lot of money on it and thought it was cool, but I wasn't having it. Needless to say, I could sense his feelings were hurt as he walked out the door.

Your Side of the Street

"Cleaning up your side of the street" basically means "control what you can control." And to break it down even more, it's about owning your shit. When you and your partner are dealing with conflict or are in the middle of an argument, all you can control is what *you* do, what *you* say, and how *you* react. That's it. As much as we ALL try to control or direct the other's feelings or actions, we can't, no matter how hard we try.

Keeping your side of the street clean is about looking in the mirror. It's about owning your own shit *without* pointing the finger back, and more than that, realizing what you can do to be a better partner or spouse.

So picture this: You and your spouse are next door neighbors. It's yard waste pickup day in your neighborhood. You've already mowed the lawn, pulled the weeds, and raked and bagged all your leaves and placed them neatly at the curb. Meanwhile, your neighbor (aka your spouse) hasn't raked up any of the leaves. The grass is long and uncut, and weeds are everywhere. Are you going to yell over the fence, "Hey Bob! Pick up your shit, dick!" No, you're not.

Sure, you can make comments like that, or you can even kindly ask Bob to pick up his shit. But ultimately, you cannot *make* good ole Bob clean up his yard. Bob'll do what he wants.

You cannot make people do, say, feel, or want what you want them to do, say, feel, or want. So what's the point in continuing to waste energy on someone else's shit when you could be using that energy to focus on your own?

Jana

I remember when I heard "your side of the street" in therapy I quickly replied, "Oh, my side of the street is shiny and clean, thank you. Next." It's easy as hell to point the finger at the other person, and I did it for years with Mike. I would always think, *Well, he's the one who fucked up, so why do I need to look on my side of the street when I've done nothing wrong?* It's a very narrow-minded response, I know, and even though, yes, I technically did nothing wrong to cause his affairs, how I handled our repair is now part of "my side of the street." You can play the blame game and point fingers for only so long. This realization was slightly annoying for me at first and took some time, but I knew the marriage wouldn't work out if I didn't put the pointer finger away and start cleaning my side of the street.

So how did I do that? What does that look like in action? How did it make me feel? How did it help us?

I was so lost when Mike was in rehab. I was scared, lonely, angry, and quite frankly all over the damn place. I didn't know what my emotions were. One day I was loving being free and ready to take on the world as a single mom, and the next day I was smashing his Xboxes and writing "asshole" on his wedding tux. Yet every day, whether I was angry or sad, I walked out to the mailbox at 3:06 p.m. because that was around the time our mailman dropped off my mail. Mike was writing me a letter each day from rehab and I clung on to those letters trying to find a sign or a glimpse of hope. Looking back, I see it now as my way of still staying close to him.

Then I joined the cast of *Dancing with the Stars*. It was the perfect opportunity to do my own thing and have a much-needed distraction. But I was in an all-out war with my emotions. Most days I would push Mike out of my brain and try to live in the world as if he didn't exist. Other days I was too weak to push and I missed him; I hoped he would be in the audience watching me perform, rooting for me. Regardless of how I was feeling, whenever he would call from rehab, I would lash out at him, tell him I didn't want anything to do with him, but the second I hung up the phone there was this pull at my heart and I hated that I missed him. The only thing that kept me calm during that time was our baby girl, Jolie. But even in her eyes I saw him, and it confused my heart even more.

One night, immediately after I'd finished doing the jive on the show, my manager Kathryn sat me down and said, "Mike filed for divorce." I thought, *HE DID WHAT?!?!* I called him, screaming, "How could you file for divorce? That's what *I'm* supposed to do. How dare you file?" He replied with "Jana, you won't let me see our daughter." It's true. When he had called asking to see her when he got out of rehab—as it had already been a little more than two months since their last visit—I said no. I was so desperate to keep close to me the one thing that brought me calm, that, even though

I knew it was wrong and would hurt him, I said he couldn't see her until after I finished filming, which could take a month.

Suddenly, thinking about raising our daughter separately and the beginning of separate parenting, separate holidays, separate everything, a voice in my heart finally spoke up in defense of this man and our marriage and Jolie. I knew what I wanted. "No," I said to him, "I want to try."

That's when the real work began. It started with me getting honest with Mike about the past few months. I had let myself have some—how should I put it?—"flirts and flings" during our separation. I told Michael about them when he asked, even though, damn, did a part of me want to lie through my teeth. If I had entertained other guys purely out of retaliation, that would be one thing; I could own that. But I know myself and I know I was genuinely intending to move on. I wanted to prove to myself that I was still loveable. He heard my truth and accepted it.

A few months after I told him, we were in therapy when he turned to me and asked for an apology. I remember sitting there thinking, *Why do I have to apologize to you? We are in this situation because of you, and I would NEVER have entertained anyone else if you didn't do what you did.* Mike would say, "Yeah, but we were still married," and I would say, "Yeah, but we were separated, because of *you*." We danced that dance for quite some time. I dug my heels in. I wouldn't apologize. But one day I realized it wasn't about the logistics. It's *never* about the logistics—the "rules" or the details or the justifications or the rationalizations. In fact, leaving all that behind will make cleaning your side of the street a much easier, smoother, and more painless process. My actions had hurt him, no matter separated or not. My actions caused him to feel a certain way, and here I was blaming him for *my* actions.

How I choose to live and the decisions I make are on me, and the same goes for Mike. Owning your side of the street is about letting go of the scorecard in your relationship and accepting that you are what you do. I have to own my actions even when it's really difficult to do so. It's a lot easier to cast blame than to look in the mirror, and *damn*, have I looked in the mirror a lot to recognize my flaws and how I can be better. And today it's by saying, "I'm sorry if my actions caused you to feel pain. I'm so sorry."

A Note About Therapy

A lot of sweat, tears, sleepless nights, and therapy have gone into achieving what we have. The latter is where we had the awakening moment of "Oh shit, this is going to be hard."

Many relationships have that "wake-up" moment after that first fight that cuts a bit deeper than before—you know, the one that really gets you thinking, "Can I do this? Is this who I want to be with?" Well, for us, it came after we started going to therapy. Now don't let that scare you away from therapy. We're huge advocates of it. The reason this was our eye-opening moment was because it was the first time both of us were willing to change our selfish ways in order to make a relationship work. We actually wanted to learn about one another, but in doing so we were faced with the perceived obstacles of compromising, adapting, and changing our ways. None of which is easy to do.

Learning how you each receive information, what makes you tick, how you each show and receive love, what your triggers are, or what your relationship needs are are all scary to consider when you realize that your relationship won't last solely on that high of new love. Or because you both believe that you're "meant to be." Therapy was the smack in the face we needed in order to understand that any relationship worth having takes work. In the past both of us just did what we wanted to do, never truly putting in the effort required for a healthy partnership. We were two of those suckers who thought that when we found the person we were meant to be with, it would be easy. Fortunately, this time, neither of us ran when things started to get hard.

Therapy stirred up a lot of shit for us, but we wouldn't be where we are today if we had never started going. It opened the doors to those fights, arguments, disagreements, and conflicts that created a learning, growing, and introspective environment. Sure, we had plenty of "oh shit" moments when it seemed overwhelming—so much so that we questioned whether we were going to make it. Everyone has those at some point; ours were the conflicts that came after we started therapy. Yours may have been after a particular argument. Whatever it was or is, don't fear it. Lean into it and use it as a springboard to take your relationship to another level and learn to fight The Good Fight.

Mike

There were so many days during the first year of our reconciliation after discovery of my affairs when we thought, *WTF is going on?* Honestly, *most* days were like that. We said so many hurtful things during those dog days. Especially me. Unfortunately, when I begin to get defensive and go into a place of shame, my initial reaction is to get mean and nasty when verbally fighting back. Which is absolutely the last thing Jana deserves after what I have already put her through. Needless to say, so many days were filled with pain, hurt, sadness, despair. There isn't an adjective in the English language that describes how hard it was or how unattainable that so-called light at the end of that tunnel seemed. But even throughout those days of misery, we were both still there. We both continued to show up, despite the fact that all it would take to end that pain was a signature at the bottom of divorce papers. We just kept showing up.

But the more therapy we went to, the more tools we learned and began practicing with one another, and the more we saw that light that once seemed unattainable. That's how we knew it was all worth it. It was never an "aha" moment. It was about getting down and dirty with one another, trudging through the darkest time of our lives.

Nowhere was dirtier during those days than my side of the street. And like every act of serious deep cleaning, sometimes it could be . . . daunting. In my case, some days it was daunting to the point of paralysis. But the promise of keeping my side of the street clean was ultimately the reason I was able to stay.

Now, some of you may scoff at my saying that I *chose* to stay. Some of you are probably thinking, "He was the one who fucked up! Why would he consider not staying?" I get it, and Jana even said that to me a time or two. But it takes work on the part of both people to make a relationship worthwhile. Granted, it took much more work on my end in the beginning in order to get us back to par. From that point on it was about both of us controlling what we could control. If Jana never had been able to own her own shit and just continuously wanted to shame me, then there is no way

I could have stayed. A person can take only so much. And sure, I hit moments when I seriously questioned whether I could stay in this. Thankfully, through Jana's hard work and dedication to her family, she was able to realize that the dynamic of our relationship has two equal and opposite forces—one I control and the other she controls. It's collaborative.

Being the "bad guy" (or "perpetrator") in our relationship added some intense extras when trying to keep my side of the street clean. Feelings of shame, guilt, sadness, and anger wanted to take over anytime I started looking at my own shit. In particular, the shame. Unfortunately, where there is shame, defensiveness tags along. Just the other day Jana and I got after it a little bit—coincidentally about taking responsibility for things from the past.

Let me explain a little more. Jana recently has been dealing with some past traumas through the use of eye movement desensitization and reprocessing therapy (EMDR). (I highly recommend EMDR; it can be extremely beneficial.) We were having a nightly check-in, as we typically do, and Jana began to vulnerably share about some events in our past that she had blamed herself for—situations where she took responsibility for my actions because of what she had been guilty of in previous relationships. (Which for the record is not healthy and goes against the concept of cleaning your side of the street. My actions are my actions, and only I am responsible for them.) When Jana started sharing her feelings, I immediately began to feel shame, which in turn became defensiveness. An internal dialogue started: *Oh here we go again, what did I do now, everything is once again my fault, I get it, I'm the bad guy. . . .* It was painful to sit in that moment. So when I began to feel overwhelmed with that shame, I did what any shame-filled person would consider the healthy thing to do—turn it around on the other person and defend. Duh.

Clearly, this is an area that I continue to work on daily. The more I practice leaning in with empathy in those moments, the better I get, but this example shows how powerfully shame and guilt can come up at any moment.

This all comes down to selfishness. It's the filter with which I listen to Jana at times. In the above example, I filtered what she was saying and focused on how it affected *me*, when really, I needed to be listening to how *she* was being affected. I had to remind myself that when she is sharing her feelings, I need to set aside what I'm feeling and focus on and receive what she is feeling. (My feelings aren't forgotten; I just need to express them at a later time.) So obviously, I had to make amends after not handling that scenario in a healthy way. I had to apologize.

Learn to Apologize

Keeping your side of the street clean means learning how to apologize the right way. Apologizing the right way means when you fuck up, you own it. It means when you say "I'm sorry," it's not followed with a "but" and then some excuse you use to justify what you did or said. We all at times blame our partners, and yeah, he probably did something that motivated you to say what you said. But it's up to your partner to apologize for what she did when it's her turn to own her side. The only thing you can control is what you say or do, so apologize for that and then leave it.

Jana had an unlimited supply of ammunition in regard to this situation. She sometimes used what I had done in the past as the reason for why she acted a certain way or said something mean. But that's on her to own and apologize for later. It's on me to keep my side of the street clean by not reacting, not fighting back, and remaining empathetic.

Jana and I continue to work at owning our own side and apologizing, and we still have moments that straight-up suck. But when it comes down to it, we're adults and we're responsible for our actions. As much as we like to say "You made me [fill in the blank]" when we're arguing, it's always totally inaccurate. You can't make anyone do anything, and no one can make you do anything.

There's nothing more effective at squashing bullshit in your relationship than a genuine apology. And it turns out there's nothing more difficult to do! So we use a three-step practice for apologizing that helps us own our shit in front of each other. Next time you have an opportunity to apologize for something, try this:

1. Say your apology: "I'm sorry about . . ."

2. Express empathy for the fact that what you said or did may have caused your partner certain feelings: "I realize when I do x it may cause you to feel y."

3. Then stop.

Yes, stop. Don't try to explain, justify, or rationalize your actions. Just sit with it, which we will warn you is very uncomfortable at first. Allow your partner to sit with it as well. Don't be discouraged by that uncomfortable silence. Let your partner be the first to say something in response. We're optimistic that your partner will receive your apology better and will be much more open to hearing your feelings if you follow these three steps.

The key to this being successful is managing your expectations. The severity of what you are apologizing for could affect how your apology is received or whether your partner is even in a place to receive it. So when you try this, which we hope you do, don't have any expectations. Don't do it for a particular reaction or expression of appreciation. Do it because you are showing that you care about your partner's feelings and are genuinely apologetic for your part.

Communicate Expectations

This takes us into another big topic around why your relationship may not be the fairy tale you had hoped for. What were your expectations going into it? What were you basing those expectations on? Were they realistic?

We all know how the dating world works. Everyone is out there trying to portray the overexaggerated best versions of themselves. We all know that's the game, and when we start to date someone, it's easy to hope, but we're naive to believe that we'll get that version day in and day out.

Say you get past that point and come back to reality understanding that we're all human and can't be our best versions every day. You still have certain expectations, don't you? Of course you do—we all do—but does your partner know what they are? Now really think about that for a minute. Have you discussed expectations for your relationship, for each other, for your future? We can tell you that we didn't have in-depth conversations about expectations in the early stages of our relationship. And we suffered because of it. The worst part of it was that we were passive in moments when we had expectations and then expected the other person to pick up on them. Great communication there, Mike and Jana!

We also had our moments of looking at the relationships of friends and comparing what we had to what they had. We've already touched on this above, but it's worth mentioning again. Social media set us up for failure when it comes to expectations and comparisons. The truth of the matter is that you never know what's going on behind closed doors. You never know what pain or unhappiness may be behind a pretty smile or a "perfect" Instagram post. Take us, for example. People used to comment on our social media accounts with #Goals, #CoupleGoals, and all that BS. That was at the beginning when they didn't know that shit was a total mess between us.

So just remember that setting expectations in your relationship based on comparison to others will not fulfill you. Be introspective, figure out your needs, and communicate your needs and expectations to the person you love. If that person loves you and is able to fulfill your needs and you can reciprocate, then you'll be happier than anyone you see on your social media feeds.

Expectations should be an open and ongoing conversation with your significant other. Talk respectfully and directly about what expectations you have in y'all's relationship. We're just talking about communication here (see Chapter 4).

Resentment Monster Hiding in the Dark

If you don't apologize and communicate your expectations, resentment can build up. Resentment is a deadly beast, and it has gotten its lethal claws into us several times throughout our relationship. It's a complex, multilayered emotion that lingers in the dark waiting to pounce. The weight of it is hard to carry in any relationship—with friends or family, romantic relationships, all of them. What's unfortunate is that it can often begin to build off of something so seamless and insignificant that you don't even realize it's there until shit hits the fan. We bring this up in this chapter because we realized that a lot of our resentments began from a "dumb fight" that resulted from focusing too long on our partner's side of the street rather than on our own.

Early on, we believed we resolved our petty arguments thoroughly by saying "I'm sorry" and then reconnecting. But truly resolving a conflict usually takes more than that. It's about using that resolution period to learn more about one another. It's about learning the steps you both need to take to avoid another experience like the one you're getting through.

Throughout our lives as individuals we learn from our mistakes, so why not do the same in our relationships? Why does that seem so difficult to do, and why do some of us keep having the same arguments over and over? We wish we had the answers for you, but we don't. All we know is that we want to stop having those same arguments over and over as much as you do. Learning more about what caused a conflict and the feelings around it on both sides has been helping us.

So we've touched on how some tiresome arguments can create resentment if not thoroughly discussed, but what about those brewing resentments that come out passively during a completely unrelated discussion?

Mike

I think of resentment as a dark figure lurking in the corners of your soul waiting for the right time to jump out and blow up a situation or even your world to shit. I look at it that way because that's what I felt like my resentments were doing. They were hiding around the corner just waiting to leap in front of me, kick me in my emotional ball sack, and yell "Gotchya!" as they proceeded to hijack my feelings.

Let me give you an example from early in my relationship with Jana that came up often. To start it off, let me say that I could hand you a hat with more than a dozen ripped-up pieces of paper in it, each with a topic of conflict, and have you pick one out. It wouldn't matter what topic you picked, but during that conflict, my resentful feelings would find a way to surface. Plug in whatever issue you want to, but ultimately, I would find a way to make a comment about it being "Jana's world" and "We have to do what Jana wants and I'm just along for the ride."

I'm sure some of you have felt this way at times. When maybe the relationship seems one-sided, or you make it up to be because of your own issues. Which is exactly what I was doing—and proves another point I want to make. That resentments aren't just created by the fault of your partner; they can manifest because of your own personal issues, interpretations, and feelings.

The reason I started making "Jana's world" comments was because when she and I first met, I was on my way out of the NFL after a five-year career, and I quickly went from "Mike Caussin, NFL Tight End," to "Mike Caussin, Jana Kramer's Husband and Former NFL Player." I lost my sense of self and identity. A lot of professional athletes struggle with that transition when they retire from their athletic careers, but the added layer for me was being married to a celebrity with a certain amount of notoriety.

Now, I loved and still love being Jana's husband, but early in the relationship I had no idea who I was anymore. I was in a new city, with a new house, living with someone (which I had never done before), with new friends around me—all while trying to transition into a life without the game I had played the previous seventeen years of my life. On top of that, I was with someone who had a very busy and rigorous travel schedule and was always on the go. She didn't have time to slow down because she was trying to keep her career moving upward.

As time went on I felt more and more insecure, I felt guilty for not bringing in any money, I felt empty without having my own professional purpose—I just felt lost. So slowly, I started to take out my own issues on Jana; it felt unfair that I had to organize my life around her schedule and what was convenient for her. But the thing is, if the roles were reversed and I were still playing football, I would have asked and expected the same from her. Both football and acting are very demanding professions; they are time-consuming and inflexible when it comes to your professional obligations.

My issues continued to grow into resentment, and time after time during arguments I would throw all that in Jana's face: "It's your world, I'm just along for the ride, blah blah blah." But really, I just didn't know how to express my issues or explain myself to her.

Ultimately, I held that against her and took it out on her. Sure, she played her part at times and probably did things that caused me to feel that my resentments were valid. Neither of us is a saint here, but it came down to my not being emotionally developed enough to express what was really going on. Through our *Whine Down* podcast and engaging with other couples who follow us on social media, I can confidently say that plenty of you have felt the same way—especially the men out there.

To finish off my thinking here, I just want to reiterate the importance of speaking your feelings. Don't do what we did and treat each other like the enemy. Lean into one another and stay ahead of these feelings before they manifest into something more. Resentments will pull you apart if you don't communicate what is weighing on your heart. Jana and I have found a game/tool that lets us clear away any festering issues with low stakes.

Last Thought for All You Men Out There

It's hard to know what's really going on with us internally at times. Society has raised men to push emotions down or aside and to "rub some dirt on it." So I get that it's difficult to express what you're feeling in a healthy way when you were never taught how to do that. This process takes time, it takes practice, and you won't get it right a lot of times at first. I still get it wrong, and sometimes it feels like I'll never consistently succeed at it, but I'm trying to change how I am. Regardless, we are responsible for our own actions and how we handle situations despite the societal influence on our upbringing.

There is a quotation I read once that has always stuck with me: "Anger is nothing more than an outward expression of hurt, fear, and frustration." When I'm having a tough time with my emotions, I think of that, and it helps me get to the root of my issue so I can try to address it and communicate it from a better place.

The one who initiates the game says, "Hey babe, have I done or been doing anything that has bothered you lately?" The key is bringing it up in a lighthearted way to create a safe environment where anything can be said as long as it's from a good place.

Once the first person shares something—let's say Jana says, "I don't like it when you leave your massive shoes in the middle of the floor"—then the person who started the game shares as well— like if I told Jana, "I don't like it when you leave water bottles and trash in my truck." The goal is to make light of the fact that your partner always leaves shoes right in the middle of the floor such that when you enter the house you trip on them and almost drop all the groceries because you don't see them. (But clearly, that has never happened in our household—eye roll.)

This really has worked for us because it doesn't come across as nagging; the lightheartedness removes the possibility of the person who is feeling aggravated overreacting (if, for instance, she trips on those shoes one more damn time), and it doesn't feel one-sided. This game creates an open invitation to bring up something of concern without the worry of how your partner might react.

So next time you have a concern that may seem nitpicky, invite your partner to play the game with you, remembering to offer him or her the opportunity to share first. You never know—this silly relationship tool could be the key to stopping a resentment that otherwise would have developed into something damaging.

Regardless of all the therapy we've done, fights we've worked through, and long emotional discussions we've had together, we still understand that sometimes dumb fights just happen and there ain't nothin' behind it. Everyone has something they are dealing with in one way or another. So people are going to have bad days, and unfortunately, sometimes loved ones at home are on the receiving end of the emotional unloading those bad days can lead to. Granted, you can say that the reason someone is having a bad day is behind their reactiveness toward you. So technically, yes, there's still something behind it, but that's on them to own and express. The difference is there's nothing behind it in terms of y'all's relationship—no underlying feelings or resentments or unprocessed emotions. Instead, it's just another shitty Tuesday at work.

Also, sometimes people have bad days for no reason whatsoever. Some days you wake up in a mood "just because," and that's okay! We're human beings, not robots. We're allowed to have bad days, lazy days, selfish days, and days when you just want to get away from everyone. There's a secret to enjoying these days to the best of your ability, though. Include your partner. This may seem difficult, depending on what kind of day you're having, but if you're willing to try, then you should. Your partner doesn't have to go on your emotional ride with you, but telling him or her candidly how you're feeling can help prevent any altercations between the two of you that day. The person receiving the information knows what the other needs and not to take anything personally. The person who needs the day can do it without any pushback or judgment from the other. You can enjoy the day you want and need in true peace. Doing this has helped us tremendously.

We hope you've found some solace in this chapter, knowing that you don't have to feel alone in the hardships that relationships bring with them. Chances are that whatever you are going through, have gone through, or are scared of going through, someone else has been there too. Whether as individuals or as part of a couple, someone most likely has tread those waters. So no matter where you are or who you are—single, dating, married, divorced, kids, no kids, young, old, gay, straight, bisexual, male, female, transgender, white, black, blue, yellow, or green—you aren't alone. Relationships are universal, and they take work no matter your background or story. So don't worry about how everyone else portrays their life; focus on creating your own modern fairy tale that makes you happy.

3 Know Your Triggers

Mike

I'm a sucker for in-app purchases. Yup, I'm that person who actually buys the in-app upgrades and extra levels for games you've likely played. I justify it in my mind over and over again: "I work hard and I enjoy these stupid little mindless addicting games, so what's the big deal?" But on a few occasions I have spent an absurd amount of money on them. My rationalization has been my justifications' partner in crime in this scenario. I believe that life is short, and what's a dollar here, a dollar there? . . . maybe a twenty now and then, and admittedly even a $99.99 upgrade? Unfortunately, team Justification and Rationalization get in the way of conscious rational thought. So I was willfully ignoring how quickly that can all add up.

One day Jana had gone over the credit card statement and brought my in-app spending to our evening check-in. She had an issue with it, and we discussed it. She pointed out that at that time, we had a lot of outgoing expenses, and we needed to prioritize our spending because every penny mattered. I agreed with her (I mean, who can defend in-app purchases when you're saving for your child's college tuition?), so we agreed that I would stop and not spend another dollar that way.

And then, a month later, I got to the point where I rejustified and rerationalized the behavior. I would liken this to those unnecessary, but comforting, trips to Starbucks or insisting on taking an Uber when the bus would work—creature comforts that are easy to rationalize but never good for the bottom line. So there I was, about to level up, thinking, *I'll just do this one and then I'll let Jana know, or maybe she won't notice because who cares anyway?*

Ultimately, Jana saw it on the credit card statement. Typically, spending money on in-app purchases would be far down on the list of things we have time to fight about. Except that we had recently agreed as a couple that I would stop this behavior, and then Jana found out I'd gone back on my agreement. The biggest issue of this was that she didn't hear it from me; she discovered it elsewhere (on the statement) . . . and that's where emotional triggers came in.

In that moment, Jana was reminded of my cheating—the number of times I told her that I wouldn't cheat again and yet I did, or the number of times she found out new information even though I had sworn to her there was nothing more to find out. So when we finally had the fight about the in-app purchases, I knew we weren't actually arguing about money. It was about cheating, lying, concealing—the last things I wanted to have another argument about but the exact trauma I had forced Jana to relive.

It's my responsibility as Jana's partner to know her triggers—to understand them, empathize with them, and avoid them when they need avoiding. Having said that, it hasn't always been easy for me to understand the correlation between the trigger and what would seem to be an unrelated situation on the surface. These scenarios have come up many times throughout the past years of our relationship repair, and I haven't handled them well. I wouldn't be able to make the connection to past triggers right away and would get extremely defensive and minimize her feelings by saying something like, "It was just a game, why is this such a big deal?"

Well, folks, triggers are indeed a big deal—your triggers and your partner's triggers—which is why we're devoting an entire chapter to knowing and owning them, and ultimately loving them.

Welcome to the Trigger Party

Until four years ago, Jana and I couldn't identify our triggers. We typically just blamed each other for pissing each other off so badly; we didn't think that the way we were feeling in a given moment had anything to do with the past, but only with what was happening in that moment. Needless to say, we were WAY off. Looking back at situations now, we almost chuckle to ourselves that we weren't able to put two and two together. It seems so obvious and clear where these triggers come from. Our biggest struggle, though, is reminding ourselves of that when we are back in the trenches taking argument grenades.

A trigger is something that sets off a memory tape or flashback that transports a person back to an earlier trauma. That being said, triggers aren't based only around traumatic events. A trigger can be any sight, smell, or sound that creates some sort of feeling or reaction in you. It can be the actions of another person, whether verbal or physical. It can even be something you read or hear that causes you to feel a certain way. You probably get triggered every day by something without even knowing it. The triggers we talk about primarily are those that create a negative, anxiety-filled reaction because those are the ones that require the most amount of work. But happy triggers do exist, and we tend to overlook the strength and power of them.

Happy Triggering

Do you ever have that moment in your day when you find yourself feeling a lot of gratitude for your partner? When you see her and think, "Wow, I'm so lucky to have her in my life," or "I love what we have"? Oftentimes, those thoughts or feelings come after those small personal or intimate moments—moments that may seem so minor to your partner, but for you they're so much more. Sure, you gain appreciation after your partner does something big and grand, but what we're talking about here is something that pulls at those heart strings in such a way that you're filled with euphoria.

Such moments are happy triggers in your relationship. Maybe it's when he comes up behind you and kisses you on the neck, causing you to feel loved, chosen, and safe. Or maybe it's when she lies on your chest in bed at night, which subdues those stresses from the day and transports you into a place of relaxation and ease. Whatever yours may be, every relationship has those moments, those happy triggers.

Think about yours. What does your partner do that stirs up those feelings in you?—the feelings that make you stop and say "Wow." Our follow-up question is, Have you shared that with your partner? If not, we highly recommend you do. It's almost like giving your partner a cheat code or a key that can unlock a part of you that only he or she can truly open. How nice would it be if your significant other, realizing you were having a tough day, could access a happy trigger and fill you with love. What a gift that is for both of you.

Jana

I've always associated triggers with negative memories of past traumas. Like the time I had to get my appendix taken out in a hospital in Romania. There was this very distinct smell in the hospital, and sometimes at the most random places I'll smell that same scent and it will send me on an emotional spiral. I go right back to the anxiety, fear, and chaos of that time in my life. And in that way even the word "trigger" can be triggering.

But here I want to focus on happy triggers.

I've only recently started to embrace them for what they are. I'm having one right now, in fact. I'm sitting at my desk in our new home. In our office Michael and I have two desks that face each other. We've been writing together on this book for the past few months, and it's been a happy time. Just being in our home, in our office, writing OUR book about our Good Fight and where we are today in this moment makes me feel calm and happy. I feel peaceful when I walk in here and start typing; the feeling has all the intensity of a traumatic trigger, but in the other direction. And in my anxious world, I'm breathing that in and letting that settle my heart. It's funny, though, because he's probably thinking right now, "Why is she smiling at me like that?"

I also have a happy place that I think all people need to have— like that scene in the movie *Something's Gotta Give* when Jack Nicholson's character is trying to calm down and he imagines a hammock under palm trees by water, and a peach margarita and Cuban cigar. For me, it's my grandma's house in Up North Michigan. When I was a kid, we spent the summers at the lake house, and to this day, when I'm having a hard time, I close my eyes and see that place and imagine I'm there. Up North, to put it simply, is magical. I've always felt free up there.

We've turned it into a family tradition now to take Jolie and Jace up there for the Fourth of July, and I remember last year just pausing and feeling so thankful. Here I was at my favorite place ever with my beautiful family. Seeing my little girl Jolie running around and sitting by bonfires with the biggest grin truly melted me and gave me a lasting happy trigger for life.

I know it may seem weird to close your eyes and picture a place you love, or a place you want to visit someday, but maybe when the traumatic triggers come up, you can take some of their power away with your happy trigger place because that's where we are the most alive. That's where we can be the most free.

Mike

Happy triggers can affect you indirectly as well. I have moments when I'm holding Jace, looking into his gray-blue eyes, which he somehow got from two brown-eyed parents, or when I'm lying in bed with Jolie reading her a book—and then a wave of emotion comes over me. The hair on the back of my neck stands up, followed by goose bumps running up my arms, finishing with some watery eyes. All due to the happy trigger of being with my kids, feeling so unspeakably blessed, grateful, and fortunate to have my family.

My wife and kids are the fuel that keeps my fire burning. My life is where it is today because of them. I'm getting emotional just writing about this happy trigger because I'm triggered right now as I write. Why I said this can trigger indirectly is because it's nothing Jana did in that moment. But I leave that moment having so much love and appreciation for her, thanks to that happy trigger of being close to our children.

I want to share another happy trigger that may seem a little un-conventional, and it's more of a topical or conversational happy trigger. I tend to have a problem communicating with "authority." I get frustrated when I'm told what to do, I get flustered when I'm peppered with questions, and I can get sour when challenged. I understand that all those things happen in a relationship, let alone a marriage, and a partnership and teamwork of any kind constantly require this kind of communication. But it can be triggering for me, sending me into a defensive place.

Here's an example of something that happened just a couple of days ago. I had been planning a potential destination fantasy football draft at our new house in Nashville. I ran the idea by Jana months and months before when our house was just in the beginning phases of being built. I even put it on our calendar: "Potential Fantasy Football Draft at House." So after polling the guys in my league, I sent them all the formal invite, and the "potential" destination draft became the "actual" destination draft.

I had some fears around bringing it up to Jana because of my own issues around being questioned. Sometimes I just want to say whatever it is I need to say and get the response, "Okay, sounds good." But Jana, God bless her, isn't built that way. She's an inquisitive, type A badass of a human being who wants to be informed because she doesn't like to half-ass anything. So I told Jana that the draft had gone from potential in status to green-light-this-shit-is-happening. I told her who all was confirmed to come, who would be taking the guest rooms, and the outline of what the weekend would most likely look like. And then I paused, did battle with the part of me that struggles to communicate, and prepared myself to get defensive. And then, the best thing happened: she basically said, "Okay, sounds good."

Jana knows my triggers; she knows my negative ones and she knows my happy ones. I hope this story illuminates the reasons why you should learn your partner's triggers, and know your own by heart. Sometimes you can improve your relationship immediately by seemingly small changes. It doesn't mean Jana can't ever challenge me on details; it means she knows when I need to hear "sounds good" and when I'm ready for all of the follow-up questions. She accepted what I told her, and in some weird, fucked-up way, it felt like she was accepting *me*.

It was a happy trigger for me. I didn't feel challenged; I felt supported and understood and loved. It's possible that nothing about that makes any sense to you, or maybe it resonates. That's the whole thing about happy triggers: they are 1,000 percent personal.

Trauma Triggers
Jana

My entire life, I dealt with triggers by running.

Running as fast and as far away as I could. It has somewhat become a "running" joke between me and Mike that I would rather move to a different country than deal with any sort of confrontation, so it made sense that I also couldn't deal with triggers. But I never really knew what they were or how they worked, especially in relation to a traumatic event.

A long-standing trigger for me stems from my first abusive marriage. I learned a lot of things the hard way in that relationship. I never stood up for myself back then; I was victimized and allowed the abuse. I got small, I tried to disappear. Coming out of that traumatic relationship I vowed that I would not allow someone to abuse and walk all over me like that again. So I ended up reacting in the way that made me feel safe in order to protect myself. Fighting back.

This was something I had never done in my life. I always took the punches because I was too scared to stand up for myself, or I wouldn't say anything and walk away because I felt I was standing in the middle of "feeling grenades" that I had a hard time processing. Sometimes I felt like I was watching myself from afar. It's a lonely place, feeling helpless, lost, and hurt. The screaming of a hurt little girl trying to be heard.

It took Mike a long time to be empathetic to my triggers, so because I didn't feel heard, I yelled louder, and that's not the way to get someone to listen to you. I wanted Mike to feel my pain and grieve with me. It took a very long time to get there because of Mike's own shame, but it also took a lot of work on my end to learn how to deal with the triggers. Over time, they don't have as much power over me; I work to stay in the present these days, to acknowledge where we are now, what we are doing today, how we are today, and how he is today. That has helped keep me from spiraling down with the traumatic triggers, and the fact that Mike has learned to lean with empathy and a softer heart, knowing the pain that I have experienced in the past.

Mike

Honestly, expressing empathy in response to traumatic triggers has been an extremely difficult concept for me to get ahold of. Which is rather unfortunate, seeing how triggers are a consistent obstacle in my marriage these days. My whole life I've had a skewed point of view about myself in relationships. I thought that if I didn't commit any obviously negative behaviors, like cheating, marriage would be easy. What a joke that was! After I went to rehab and then Jana and I reconciled, I thought that as long as I wasn't cheating, we would be able to build trust in our relationship. Wrong! That was a ridiculous myth that I used to believe and that came from an unempathetic frame of mind.

At the beginning of our reconciliation process, it was difficult to maintain the empathy that Jana needed when she was triggered. It happened more frequently, she was harsher with her words toward me, and at times there didn't seem to be an end in sight to this pain. When I reached my limit of empathy, I would get defensive and say things like, "Well, I'm not cheating *now!*"—basically different ways of saying to her, "Get over it." I was so selfish that I wanted to try to rush Jana's process of grieving for the past and redirect her focus to the present.

I was doing that because I couldn't handle sitting in the uncomfortable shame of my own actions. It was easy for me to forget the past and focus on the present because I didn't want to be reminded of how much of an asshole I had been. Anytime we talked about the past, I went into a deep place of shame. And when you're stuck in shame, it's very difficult to consider someone else's feelings, let alone put those feelings ahead of your own. It took a lot of work for me to get to the place where I could sit and listen to Jana while putting my own feelings and triggers aside. I had to stop focusing on trying to save face. Jana needed to be heard, she needed me to grieve with her, because traumatic triggers take significant time to understand and process. Unfortunately, they never really go away. That said, over time and with a lot of work, their effect on a person doesn't carry the same weight.

These days the triggers from Jana's past trauma still occur, but they look different. They don't have the same impact they used to have. Not because they are any less painful, but because of the work Jana and I have done individually and together. For me, I've learned how to not run away from that pain anymore. I've learned how to stand in it and even stay ahead of it at times. That means that if I foresee a situation that could be triggering for Jana, I'll address it before she has to. That shows her that I'm conscious of her feelings and not naive about the hurtful actions of the past.

If something comes up that I don't anticipate, I've gotten a lot better at being able to quickly jump into the place of empathy first, regardless of what my personal feelings may be. That's become easier primarily because of the work Jana has done, learning to express her triggered feelings without shaming or being hurtful.

These traumatically triggered feelings will never go away. So if you're in a similar situation, don't try to fool yourself into thinking that they will. I'm finally at peace with this realization. I realize the magnitude of my past addictive behaviors and actions, and I'm willing to keep getting better at being empathetic for my wife.

Triggers Suck

We've learned some very helpful tools over the years through our work with therapists that we want to share with you. First is being able to identify triggers. This is all about being introspective and acknowledging feelings when they arise. Which isn't easy. But we've learned that when something creates a feeling in us or invites a reaction, we act without acknowledging the root or cause. It may not have been anything in that moment; it could easily have been something from earlier in the day or another time that we just never addressed.

Once we started being able to stay current with our feelings, or in "real time," as therapists often say (see more on this in Chapter 4), we noticed a shift in how we communicated and reacted toward one another. That's the thing about triggers: by not communicating your feelings around something that may seem minor, that "minor" thing could possibly transform into something much more harmful to you and your relationship: resentment. By being proactive and honest about your feelings in real time, you're saving yourself from the added stress, anxiety, and pain that come along with the negativity of resentment.

Talking through triggers is so much easier said than done. Our therapists have said over and over that when dealing with triggers we need to "just breathe" or "pause and take a breath." Yeah, because it's that f'n easy. We got so sick of hearing that, because it sounds so simple but it's damn near impossible in the moment. But that was consistently their answer to a lot of our questions, so finally we figured there must be something to it and decided to start practicing it.

Through that initially painful trial-and-error phase, we realized that there indeed was something to this—just breathe, pause and take a breath. We both started to experience shifts in our energy. If we gave ourselves a moment to recenter, then we had a much better chance of acting like rational human beings. We realized that if we can speak from a calm place and express to one another how the other's action, or this memory, or that song, or something we saw triggered a past hurt, then the other could receive from a much better place. Instead of feeling attacked, the recipient would tend to feel more empathy than defensiveness. Which in turn would allow the triggered person to feel heard. Which is ultimately what that person needs.

Being able to acknowledge the deeper issue of a traumatic situation takes time, patience, and practice. Once you begin to get on that path of handling it well, it becomes easier to cut straight to those triggering feelings. It's incredibly painful for both parties to navigate these triggered feelings during the early stages. To shift in the direction of change, it's initially up to the "perpetrator," that is, the "bad guy," as Mike said earlier, who is the person who said or did something that triggered the other person. The "victim," or the person who is experiencing the trigger, needs and deserves more time before she is capable of expressing her feelings in an adult way. The victim is traumatically triggered, so she isn't in a rational mindset.

Our advice to perpetrators is simple but difficult to do: place your partner's feelings and needs ahead of your own. Again, this is simple but hard. The natural initial reaction of most people is to examine their own feelings, but in this case, you need to make sure your partner feels heard and that you show empathy. Victims are reacting to raw, unprocessed emotions—which is difficult for anyone to listen to, so it's imperative that perpetrators recall their actions in these moments. Not for the purpose of shaming themselves, but for the practice of empathy toward their partner whom they hurt so severely. Only when victims start to feel safe through the consistent actions of support and empathy from the perpetrators can they begin to acknowledge their triggers from a healthier mindset. Which allows them to explain and articulate their feelings in a more grounded manner.

We heard an example from a therapist that we like to refer to when talking about this particular situation. Imagine the perpetrator and the victim get into a car wreck. The victim's legs are broken because of the accident, which was the perpetrator's fault. If you were that perpetrator, would you look at the victim and say, "Come on! Let's go, you're fine!" Hell no! You would carry them, and cater to them, and help them in every way that you could. We think back on this example often in our own relationship because it is a great tool to use to ground ourselves.

Okay, enough of our preachy therapist talk, because even four years after first learning all this, it is still a constant practice for us. Some moments are more triggering than others. Some emotions are stronger than others, and as we all know, some days are just fucking harder than others. It's life, and life is damn hard. We remind ourselves of this in order to grant ourselves some grace in the midst of difficult situations. We know that we're doing the best we can and that at the end of the day we're committed to working through life together.

Remember, with all the pain that situations like this can cause, you're still fighting for each other; you're still fighting The Good Fight.

"Yup . . . I'm Fine"

Another phrase that we have talked about and dealt with a lot in our relationship is "validated fears." Validated fears are based around expectations you may have of your partner and managing (or trying to manage) his reaction to something.

Here's an example: Say your spouse has been doing something that really bothers you and brings up a lot of negative feelings for you. You've hesitated talking to her about it because you're afraid of her reaction. Once you finally do approach her about it, she gets defensive and takes it personally, which causes a fight, or she walks away in anger, dismissing your feelings. Your spouse just validated your fears, so you most likely won't feel safe bringing up other issues in the future.

Relationships tend to get into a pattern of validated fears. We're certainly guilty of it. This pattern can result in people holding in and not expressing their feelings, leading to increased resentment and disconnection. How many times have you and your partner had a dialogue like this?

"Hey babe, how're you doing?"
"I'm fine."
"Is everything okay?"
"Yup."

The person who is being short in this dialogue could be responding that way because of his significant other previously validating his fears. He may have come to his partner with feelings he wanted to share, but his partner got defensive and reacted negatively. Over time, this can cause anyone to bottle those feelings up.

Validated fears can be packaged many different ways, and they are always difficult to work through. We're constantly working at this still to become more consistent with each other. One of our therapists gave us some great guidance in dealing with sensitive topics that could lead to negative reactions: approach the conversation from a lighter direction. When you jump right into what is bothering you about your partner, that can feel like finger-pointing, which naturally gets anyone into a defensive frame of mind. Instead, set the stage for a conversation. Start by expressing that you are coming from a good place and that you don't want to fight. Then state your fears about bringing up the topic you need to talk about. Literally say, "I'm afraid that when I bring this topic up, you'll react negatively and defensively." Then go into how the issue makes you feel; don't go straight into what your partner did wrong. Leading with how you feel creates a more inviting environment and is easier for your partner to hear. If you lead with what your partner did wrong, that's finger-pointing again.

We've found that it's a lot easier for the receiving party to react empathetically when we approach a sensitive subject this way. Now the partner on the receiving end may not like what she hears and will most likely have her own feelings about it, but it's important for her to NOT validate the fears you lead with. She will have the opportunity to express her feelings at a later time.

Triggers from the Past

Lots of people have experienced some sort of traumatic event in their lives—sometimes during their childhood, or sometimes in relationships with others. Something happened that shaped who they are and how they are in relationships. We all remember being kids and learning that a fire is hot. All it took was that one burn to learn our lesson.

Often, that same lesson applies to trauma in relationships. We carry that feeling of getting burned by someone into the relationships that follow, and why wouldn't we? That pain sticks with us, and we adapt and act accordingly in order to avoid that pain in the future. At the same time, we know it's not fair to the new person in our lives. So how do you know when to take the leap and trust that this new person won't validate your fear of being burned again?

We've both experienced this, and we get it—it's damn hard to put yourself out there in such a vulnerable way when getting to know and trust someone new. But from our experience, we know that there is no benefit to holding on to your wounds from previous relationships. If you do, all that results is miscommunication and false expectations. How does this new person in your life really get to know you if you don't share with him where you've been?

Triggers are inevitable in any relationship. The thing to remember is this: when dealing with the baggage of past relationships and trauma, you're not alone. So don't act like you are. Bring your partner in with you so she or he can help you navigate those triggers. You're in this battle together. Emotional baggage is kind of like debt. When you marry someone, you take on his or her debt, and the same goes for emotional baggage. Now it's yours, too, and you're in the fight. But you're fighting The Good Fight for each other, fighting to repair, and fighting to bring safety back into the relationship.

4 Start Talking

Mike

For Halloween 2015, we hosted a big neighborhood party and spent two months decorating and preparing for it. Neither of us had ever been big Halloween people, so we decided to embrace it for the first time and go all out. We had a costume contest, a ton of people came, and there was plenty to drink. I had given Jana a heads-up a week before that I planned on drinking a lot and so not to expect much help from me cleaning up the next morning. If she waited until the afternoon, I would be more than willing to help.

But the thing with Jana is, she's a rise-and-shining go-getter who tackles the day from the minute she wakes up till the minute she goes to bed at night. Me, on the other hand, I love to indulge my lazy side. I'm pretty sure she doesn't know the meaning of the word "lazy" or the term "sleeping in."

Anyway, the morning after came to me with a colossal hangover. While I began to come to, I could already hear Jana single-handedly cleaning the entire house. Who knew someone so small could sound like a herd of elephants! Even though I typically would have massive anxiety about not helping, I stayed in bed because I—for once!—had communicated with Jana and asked for what I needed.

Then Jana started coming in and out of the room. I felt that her purpose was to entice me to get up and help. I stood my ground, however, and stayed in bed while I recounted and regretted every drink from the night before. Eventually I asked her, as she trudged through the room again, if everything was okay. She replied with a sharp "Yup," and I knew passive-aggressive Jana like the back of my hand at that point.

Eventually, I'd had enough. I insisted that she tell me what was going on, and no surprise, she explained that she wished I had gotten out of bed to help her clean the house. In that moment, my biggest fear was validated—that is, for once, I had communicated my feelings ahead of time, but it still hadn't mattered. I felt like my feelings and needs weren't important to her. So I did the dumbest thing possible: I escalated the situation. I said, "Are you fucking kidding me?!" And then it got ugly—lots of name-calling and yelling and door-slamming, and, well, you get the idea.

The fallout from that fight lasted for days, if not longer. It's sad to look back at that scenario now and realize how simple it could have been to work through and how much better I could have handled things. At the end of the day, we both just wanted to be heard, we both wanted to feel as though our needs mattered and our feelings were validated. Regardless of what I had asked for in advance, the house was a disaster that morning. Of course Jana wanted to clean—who would want to live in that mess? And anyone who has ever cleaned a house after a party knows that the only thing worse than the cleaning is cleaning alone while your partner is in the other room passed out or watching television.

The heart of this Halloween nightmare was communication—not doing enough of it, and doing it in all the wrong ways.

Almost any time you search, read, or hear about "the most important things for a good relationship," communication is on that list. It may even top it. But what does good communication even look like? We all hear about it, we talk about it, we all usually agree that the communication in our own relationships could be better. But how?

Before we get to how to do it better, however, maybe you'd like to hear Jana's side of the story . . .

Jana

We'd been decorating the house since September. Our walls were decked out with sheets and fake hand prints with blood, candles were everywhere—I mean it looked like a real-life haunted mansion. The party was a huge success, yet I still had a hard time letting go and having fun because I couldn't stop thinking about how I was going to clean every nook and corner of the spider webs that we had spent more than a month separating and laying out to make our house look like a spider web. Oh, and the fact that my friend HAD to wear sparkles. So she left about a dozen pounds of sparkle dust on the floor throughout the house.

Cut to eight in the morning. Mike is still passed out in bed, and I'm already an hour into cleaning up. It wasn't even nine by the time EVERYTHING was put away. It took us more than a month to decorate, but I managed to clean and box it all up within two hours. Mind you, all while being seven and a half months pregnant. Now, I do remember Mike saying he was going to help out later, but still, a part of me kept thinking, "Surely he'll hear the vacuum, and surely he'll get out of bed to help me."

But I was wrong. So I cleaned faster and more vigorously as my anger grew. So after I had finished cleaning and hauling the boxes upstairs, which I shouldn't have even done, I walked into our room and let the passive-aggressive comments fly.

Weeks leading up to this party, Mike had told me what he needed and expected. But for some reason, I hadn't accepted that. I didn't listen to what he needed or wanted in that moment. I just selfishly thought, "I'm pregnant, so of course he'll help me when I start cleaning." But I should have had a healthier dialogue with myself and said, "Okay, Jana, you have two options. You can either wait until he's ready to help, OR you're going to have to clean the entire house by yourself and not resent it."

Now, if I really had wanted his help, I could have come to him from a good place. I could have first acknowledged what he had told me and validated that I had understood what he had asked for and needed going into that day. I could have followed that up with expressing my desire to have his help and that I admittedly was doing more than I should have been doing that far along in my pregnancy. Regardless of my validating his feelings and then expressing mine, the key would be trying to have no expectations regarding his response. He still could have declined to help, and that would have been his right to do so. Sure, I probably still would have been pissed off, which is also my right, but again, he had asked for what he needed ahead of time, and I would have to respect that.

One more thing to note here, and this is something that both Mike and I have heard repeatedly from our therapists: avoid using the word "but." When you're trying to validate your partner's feelings, it's important that he or she feel heard. Using the word "but"—as in, "I hear you, but . . . "—can immediately derail your objective.

The First Step

If we could go back to the beginning of our relationship and start over, knowing what we know now, we definitely would. Not just so we could have implemented all of this good advice sooner, but so we could have a lot more conversations around basically everything.

Like most relationships, early on we fell into the trap of the "honeymoon phase," where all we did was try to please one another, because it's so tempting to relax into the good vibes and happy moments and forget that eventually real shit starts to hit the fan and you kinda need to know who's going to be fending off the shit with you. But we were never expressing any sort of relational needs, wants, or expectations. We were just flying by the seat of our pants, feeding off of that "new love" energy that seemed unbreakable and perfect. At that same time we were creating unsustainable expectations while dismissing our own needs for longevity. We'll give you an example.

Mike

Early in our relationship, I gave Jana all of my time. We spent every minute together, every single day. Which I greatly enjoyed, and I wanted to do that just as much as she did. Unfortunately, that set a standard that I knew I wouldn't be able to maintain over the course of our relationship. I never communicated with her how important it is that I have time for myself. I've always enjoyed "me time" so that I can recharge and recenter (I'll return to this in Chapter 10).

But after an incident of infidelity on my part very early in our relationship, I fell into rescue mode, and it was extremely difficult to express what I needed after I had hurt her. I felt so much shame about what I had done that I didn't believe my needs were important, or worse, I felt I didn't deserve to have any needs. As time passed, I felt increased guilt about needing space at times. I didn't want to express that need to her for fear that she would take it as choosing something else over her. So instead of being confident in my need and starting the relationship off with more realistic expectations, I just continued the way we had been.

The takeaway here is that regardless of what other events occurred in our relationship to make this an issue, I still could have come from a good place and expressed to Jana the importance of having time for myself. I could have reassured her that it had nothing to do with not wanting to be around her, and everything to do with my desire to focus on me—with the goal of being better to everyone around me.

But instead of doing it that way, I spent years holding that in, eventually producing resentment. It was like I was blaming her for the fact that I wasn't getting what I needed, even though she had no idea what I needed. I know, stupid, right?

Back to Communication . . . But How?

This example mentions "coming from a good place" and expressing needs and feelings to your partner. That sounds great, but how do you do that? We use the Safe Talk Process. The condensed version is called the Short Safe Talk Process, in which our amazing therapists, Bill and Laurie Lokey, shortened the longer, more in-depth model of Lynn Stevens. Then we changed the Lokey's version in a way that connected with us the most. We'll show you the model first and then give you an example to illustrate how we use it:

What I saw or heard _____ (the facts or behavior)

The meaning it had for me _____ (the story I made up in my head is . . . my belief is that . . .)

What I feel or felt _____ (glad, sad, angry, hurt, scared, lonely, shame, guilt)

History _____ (This reminds me of _____ from my childhood. This might link back to _____, I experienced similar
feelings when _____.)

Mike

Often, Jana will do things that cause me to play out the scenario
of role reversal in my head, that is, basically asking myself, "If I
did what she just did to me, how would she have reacted?" In the
past I usually would wait in the weeds for the perfect time to make a
verbal strike, solely motivated to prove a point. Now I try to use
the Safe Talk Process instead.

Here's an example. I'm sure any guys reading this can relate to
it, and I'm almost positive any gals reading this have been on the
receiving end. Jana was out of town for a few days for some music
gigs—I believe it was three days. Definitely long enough to miss
each other. I anticipated that the night she got home she would
want to hang out and connect, which typically she does. Hell, even
I wanted to after a few days, and I was looking forward to it.

Soon after getting home she informed me that some of her girl-
friends were coming over to play cards. I was a bit surprised and
taken aback, but I said, "Okay, no problem." Then as I began
to really digest the situation, that story-telling part of my brain
started churning, telling me that if I had done that to her, she
would have lost her shit! She would have gone into a whole tailspin
of feeling not chosen, calling me selfish, claiming I didn't care
about her, and on top of that getting upset that I didn't give her
a heads-up or even discuss it with her. All of which is, honestly,

probably true. BUT, I never allowed her the opportunity to express her truth. Instead, I held on to it until it came out sideways during an unrelated argument.

Here's how I could have handled this situation in a way that would have given both of us the chance to speak our truths: *"Hey babe, I know you just told me that your girls are coming over to play cards. But the story I've started making up in my head is about equality. I believe that if I were to do this same thing to you, you would have gone into a tailspin of emotions. What I feel right now is a bit of anger mixed with hurt. And I've experienced similar feelings in other situations during our relationship when something doesn't seem fair in my mind. Are you willing to share with me any thoughts and feelings you may have around this?"*

This is a lot more than "Okay, no problem," but it invites the opportunity to stop resentment from growing. This approach definitely has been helpful for us, and there's proof in this pudding. We've experienced a significant change in our communication by using this model. And we're not embarrassed to bring out the laminated guidelines of the Safe Talk Process to help us through.

Don't Forget

You can have the best teachers, the best therapists, and the best tools, but if you aren't mindful about these next few topics, then you're basically bringing a sword to a gunfight. Before you begin the Safe Talk Process, we believe it's imperative that you pay attention to these four areas:

GOAL: When our therapists asked us, "What is your goal?" at times we initially didn't know how to answer it. So they helped us out and gave us a multiple-choice question: "Are you trying to be right? Or trying to be heard?" We both admit that at times we weren't sure what we wanted more. Ultimately, we realized that being heard is what we most yearned for, and we bet you feel this way too. Sometimes, just verbalizing this can help make communicating easier for both parties.

YOUR BODY: It's so easy to let our energy during a particular day carry us from one task to another without ever allowing a transitional period or appropriate shift in that energy. So before we approach a potentially controversial conversation, we take a moment to notice any physical sensations that may be coming up. We have greatly underestimated the power of this and have learned more about ourselves in those moments when we take the time to sit with ourselves.

TONE: We've all had those text conversations when the tone of the conversation can feel two different ways depending on what end you are on. (For that reason alone we try to avoid having any serious conversations via text.) We look at tone as being the first impression of a conversation. You get only one first impression, right? It's just like meeting someone in person for the first time—if it doesn't start off right, then you have even more work to do in order to get back to neutral. It's the same in conversations regardless of whether you know someone. So if we go into the Safe Talk Process with an uninviting tone, we can ruin that opportunity to be heard or feel connected.

PURPOSE: This is something you need to answer for yourself. What is your purpose for using the Safe Talk Process model, or having that kind of conversation at all? For us, our purpose is fairly universal. And it has to do with at least one, if not all four, of these reasons: for connection, for understanding, to show your heart, and to lean in. Knowing that these are our purposes for these conversations starts us off on the right foot before we even open our mouths—because going into it, we know the reasons the other person wants, too.

Jana

Mike was in town visiting me while I shot a Christmas movie in Louisiana, and he had to go to my trailer to record our *Whine Down* podcast since our producer was also in town. While he did this, I was on set filming; and after a few hours I had a break, so I went to the trailer to hang with Mike. When I got there, he and the producer were packing up, so I got excited that I was about to hang with my husband since I hadn't seen him for eleven days. When I got called back to set, he said, "Alright I'm gonna head back to the apartment." I immediately said, "Oh, okay." He responded with, "Is that not okay?" I, of course, said it was fine, but what I wanted to say was, "No, it's not fine, choose me."

In Mike's defense, he had just flown in that day from Nashville, and it was about ten o'clock at night. But I thought that he wanted to hang with me, so when he said he was leaving, I was really bummed. But I played passive and gave him a half-hearted kiss goodbye. I then took my passive attitude with me to text him, which is one of the worst ways to communicate. I texted how it would have been nice if he had stayed on set and wanted to see me film and spend time with me. He texted back that he was tired and would visit another time but that he didn't want to sit around on set, which hurt my feelings again. The key thing he texted, though, was, "You didn't say you wanted to hang out." I truly didn't know I had to say that. I thought that was always a given, but in that moment, sure, I also wanted to be chosen.

Here's how we could have communicated better:

Version A:

Jana: You guys are already done recording?

Mike: Yeah, we wrapped up and now I'm going to head back because I'm tired.

Jana: I bet you're so tired from traveling, but if you're up to it, it would mean a lot to me if you stayed and hung out for a few.

Mike: Yeah, definitely, baby, I'll hang out for a few.

WOW. Fight avoided.

Version B:

Why another version? Because maybe a feeling of not feeling chosen needs to be expressed. Here's how you could do that from a good place:

Jana: I bet you're so tired from traveling. But the story I'm making up in my head right now is that you don't want to hang with me. I feel like you're not choosing me, so I feel sad and hurt, which reminds me of the past pain in our relationship.

Coming from that vulnerable place allows you to speak your feelings and not be passive, and it gives your partner a way to lean into you. Now, Mike may choose to stay, but he might also say, "I'm sorry you don't feel chosen, and that's not how I want you to feel at all because I *do* choose you—but I'm just too tired right now." At that point, though, I would have felt better regardless because I had expressed how I felt and hadn't held on to the negative feelings.

Some of you are probably thinking, *Let the poor man go to bed!* So how's this?

Mike: Baby, I'm so tired and I really want to go to bed. But I promise I'll come hang on set with you this week.
Jana: Okay, baby, get some sleep, I love you!

I could have communicated that I wanted to spend time with him. Unfortunately, I wanted to be chosen, and I didn't want to have to "ask him to do the dishes"—like the infamous scene in *The Break-Up*. I wanted him to "want" to do the dishes.

And let's be honest: in Mike's situation, the poor guy just wanted to go watch an episode of *The Office* and go to sleep. Since it's a teaching moment, though, he at least could have communicated that he wanted to spend time with me but that he was too tired.

This is exactly why using a tool like the Safe Talk Process can be so beneficial. It eliminates, or at least minimizes, the moments when you may feel like you have to be a mind reader. What we've found is that doing all that and keeping it in real time has given us the best possible scenario for success. It has helped us avoid those misses that all couples have.

Keeping It in Real Time

So what does "real time" mean, exactly? For us, it's about staying verbally current with your feelings—especially when those feelings have to do with feelings toward your partner. We understand any hesitation that you may be having with this. It may seem silly to bring your partner in on every little thought or feeling that comes into your head in that moment. We aren't saying that you have to share *every*thing. It's up to you to decipher which feelings carry enough weight to manifest into more than just initial annoyance. Especially in the early stages of a relationship, we're all less likely to bring any of these feelings to our partner.

When *is* the best time? Figuring this out is tricky because you don't want to feel stupid. It's also terrifying because you're being vulnerable, and the last thing you want is for your partner to tease you, minimize, or even dismiss your feelings. The key is all about how you propose it. Being in real time and letting your partner know right after she or he does or says whatever it is that bothers you is the primary option. We've learned through our therapy that it's more adult and healthier to be in real time. Early on, when we were practicing this, we would still get defensive with each other and weren't always in the right head space. But it gets better.

Another option is to wait for a later time that feels more neutral and bring it up then. Again, it's all about how you approach it. One strategy is this: "Hey [insert adorable pet name], are you open to learning something about me?" This approach will immediately soften your partner and promote a learning opportunity as opposed to distributing blame. He or she won't feel the need to put up a sword and a shield.

It's imperative that you lead with this kind of soft opening as opposed to something like, "Hey, can we talk?" Or even more direct, like "Why do you do____?" Here, you run the risk of your partner going straight to defensiveness. Typically, people primarily receive "Can we talk?" as "I did something wrong and he/she wants to talk to me about it." We both admittedly hear it that way.

Using the soft approach invites your partner to learn something about you, which is the goal. So why not control the situation the best you can by creating a safe learning environment? When we do this with one another, we have such a warm, connected feeling afterwards. The listener is open to accommodating the sharer's needs and embraces those needs in order to establish greater connection.

Here are some examples of what we're talking about.

Mike

Those of you who follow Jana on social media probably know that the kitchen is my domain in the household. I'm the cook in the family, so I get fairly territorial when it comes to certain things in the kitchen. Two (of the many) pet peeves I have when it comes to the kitchen are when fruit is put in the refrigerator still in plastic bags and when pots, pans, or knives are placed in the dishwasher.

For a while I never said anything to Jana about either of these. But I found myself cursing to myself at times when I saw her doing them. After some time I noticed that it was really starting to bother me, and I would become agitated with Jana, saying to myself, "Why the fuck is she doing this? Doesn't she know I hate this?" Then I realized, how would she know that these things bother me? I had never told her, or never told her in a clear way. It was solely up to me to manage my feelings by teaching her something about myself.

So instead of just saying, "Hey can you take the fruit out of the bags when you put them in the fridge?" next time she did it I approached it the way we discussed above. I asked her whether she was open to learning something about me. She responded, "Of course." So I told her about the fruit and also the pots, pans, and knives—in a kind manner. She responded with, "OMG, I never knew that."

This is an example of something so silly that it might not make sense to Jana, but because I approached it the way I did, she was able to hear me from a good place. She was willing to respect my feelings no matter how silly they may have seemed to her. On top of that, she didn't laugh at my request or make me feel stupid, so I felt safe in expressing my feelings. Which invites more vulnerability into the relationship.

Again, folks, I have hundreds of stories about how I did stuff wrong over the course of our relationship, but we think it's important to share some of our wins, too. We want y'all to feel inspired and willing to change however you have to in order to make your current or future relationship work. Again, we aren't experts, we do NOT have this all figured out, but damn, we're trying our asses off to live this life together. That's what we want, and that's how we're choosing to live.

Jana

Mike and I were having one of those playful conversations after I had finished filming for the day—romantic, sexy, funny banter back and forth mixed with a bit of sarcasm, of course. Never in my wildest dreams did I think the conversation had a chance of turning to the dark side, but somehow Mike and I always find a way.

We started to talk about scheduling, and honestly, in the moment I was still wanting to be playful, and even though I wasn't bothered by his talking about it, I said, "Well, let's talk about that later, although you know I always fold." As soon as "fold" came out of my mouth, a dark cloud entered the bed and breakfast where we were staying. Then, unbeknownst to me, I continued to dig a hole into a larger mess, elaborating on how I fold. Like how I had agreed to eat at Chili's for dinner one night even though I would have rather eaten dirt, but I wanted to make him happy; or how I had agreed to travel to his parents' house for Christmas (which is another long story in itself). Mike started to shut down, but I just kept defending how and why I fold because he seemed so shocked that the words "I fold" had even come out of my mouth.

Then he walked out of the room, and about thirty minutes later he came back to talk to me. I could tell he was upset, and I give him a million high fives for trying to talk to me from a good place. He told me that he had been really triggered and that he wanted to talk to me about why he felt that way and the root of it.

To give you a little backstory: As we've told you, our relationship happened really fast after Mike and I met. We moved in with each other within a few months, and I remember it like it was yesterday that we got into the fight that has seemed to always come back to bite me in the ass. We were living together in the house we had just bought, and shortly after that I told him, "I don't want to just play house." And I didn't. I was serious. We started talking about getting engaged, and he said he could wait. "How long can you wait?" I asked him, and he answered, "I don't know, maybe five years."

To me, he might as well have put a death sentence on my ovaries. I was thirty years old at the time and scared of that ticking biological clock. I was very clear with Mike when I met him that I wanted kids and I wanted to get married, sooner rather than later. So when he said five years, I went a little bit nuts. I didn't go crazy, but I was direct. And that moment when I said, "I don't want to just play house" has been one of our favorite arguments from our past to bring up and rehash. For Mike, it represents my asking him to do something before he was ready, in order to please me. For me, it's a moment of standing my ground and speaking my truth and then being made to feel pushy, nagging, and controlling because of it.

Back to Louisiana: Michael brought up that exact "I don't want to just play house" moment from our past in order to illustrate why hearing me say "I always fold" made him shut down. It confused him, and he was trying to express his feelings. But I couldn't hear any of that. Hearing this past fight brought up at a moment when I didn't want to be fighting sent my emotions spiraling. *Here we go again*, I thought, and I went to my trigger of hearing the "just play house" story and thinking Mike was going to throw it in my face.

Luckily, Mike fought better than me in that moment. I'm proud of his resolve. After I realized he wasn't trying to bring up bad memories and was just trying to say how he felt, we were able to have a very calm and healthy conversation. Winning!

Mike

Jana painted the picture well for y'all. We honestly can't even remember what we were talking about that day in Louisiana that started this all. She says it had to do with scheduling, but I don't remember what "I always fold" was about. Ultimately, it didn't matter. Once she said that, that's all I could focus on.

Let me give you two reasons why that comment is triggering for me. Jana told you about the "just play house" conversation, and that unfortunately was a situation that I resented during the early years of our relationship. As I saw it, I had just moved my entire life to a new state for her, bought a house with her (even though I still had one in Baltimore), and was doing everything I could to show her I was serious about this relationship and I wanted to spend my life with her. I had never lived with another woman before, and here I was moving and buying a house with her. I was all in.

October 2014 we closed on the house, and in November she made the "just play house" comment. We had that fight, and what I heard was that everything I had just done to express my commitment to her wasn't enough. I never said that I didn't want to get married or didn't want to have kids because I reassured her that I wanted both. All I said was that I could wait. In my opinion, it just didn't have to be a conversation only two months after I had moved there and one month after we had bought a house. Why this relates to "not folding" is because that moment felt like an ultimatum.

The second example I mentioned to her was about Christmas. That's a stressful time for everybody. Trying to make family, friends, and loved ones all happy on both sides is very difficult. My mom had made a comment to us once about wanting us to "come home every year for Christmas." Jana took it very literally and told me that, no, she couldn't see us doing that. I was caught in the middle trying to please both parties. I told Jana that I didn't want to go back to my family for a few years because I wanted to start our own holiday traditions just as much as she did. At the same time, I wasn't going to shut the door on the possibility of going to Virginia for Christmas down the road. When my mom made that comment, I let it go in one ear and out the other, like most kids do with their parents, no matter how old they are. I just knew that one day I would like to take the kids to Grandma and Grandpa's for the holidays.

In recent years Jana has offered to go to Virginia for Christmas, but honestly, I didn't believe her offer was genuine because of how unwavering she had been earlier. That's why when she said that she "always folds," I was triggered. It was one of those moments when you hear your partner say something that paints a picture of your life in complete opposition to what you see as reality.

I'm not talking of one of those moments when you may be on the fence and begin to question yourself. No, it's that moment when your flag is planted in the ground and no amount of persuasion can change your perspective. It can be infuriating, and it has happened to all of us. Maybe it's the guy who always says "We never have sex" or it's the gal who says "You never plan anything" when your version of reality is that you're doing the best you can. Hearing Jana generalize in that way was jarring and painful.

My whole purpose for reminding Jana of those situations was to show her why I was triggered by what she said. Those were two situations in which she showed no promise of compromise, let alone folding. They were two scenarios that caused lingering rifts in our relationship. Fortunately, I've worked through them both and gotten to a good place with them. I don't have those same resentful feelings anymore. Which is primarily why I was able to keep my emotions in check and come back to Jana from a good place. It was a learning moment for both of us, and we deserved to be excited about handling that situation the way we did.

The main reason we were able to avoid catastrophe in that situation is that we kept it in real time; that is, we dealt with it in the moment and didn't give it a chance to linger and manifest as a stronger emotion that would come out sideways later during a completely irrelevant discussion. And my taking that thirty-minute timeout still kept it in real time—those thirty minutes were a real-time chance for me to process my emotions. So next time you feel something come up in a discussion, speak on it. Use it as a learning tool for your relationship. Jana and I did, and we walked away together without added scars and as a more unified front.

Checking In

It doesn't get more real time for us than checking in. Checking in is a perfect opportunity to share what's going on with you, while on neutral ground, we might add. It's the best tool we have in our toolbox when it comes to staying in real time. We do a nightly check-in that we call FANOS:

Feelings

Affirmations

Needs

Own

Sobriety

Feelings is about what you've been feeling recently, that day or even in that moment. You don't have to elaborate on the feelings unless you want to. Sometimes we enjoy just stating how we feel without explanation. It's freeing to not feel like you have to either explain or defend why you feel the way you do.

Affirmations is about your partner. You give that person affirmations on things that you have experienced or seen him or her do. It can be anything from "Thank you for taking out the trash" to "Thank you for coming into the kitchen and giving me a hug and kiss out of nowhere" to "Thank you for all the hard work you do for this family." It can be anything. Even "Thank you for not reacting when I was being bitchy earlier." It's about acknowledging your partner for anything he or she did that affected you in some way.

Needs focuses on you. What do you need from your partner that day, night, or week? "I need a little bit more affection from you this week," or "I have a crazy work week coming up, so I really need your support and understanding." Those are two examples of keeping it in real time by preparing your partner for what's coming up. We don't always communicate every detail of our lives with our partner, so how is he supposed to know, for instance, that you have a busy and stressful week coming up? Or how does she know you need some more affection? Instead of expecting our partner to read our minds, we have this great opportunity to express our needs to him or her so we don't unfairly hold negative feelings.

Own is straight-up calling yourself out: "I'm sorry for being a dick/bitch yesterday." You get the point. This is a great way to have some checks and balances in your relationship. If you're able to call yourself out, then the narrative changes a bit instead of your partner having to "nag" you.

Sobriety. This one is for us specifically, but anyone dealing with addiction might find it helpful to implement. We share our therapy schedules and plans coming up. For us, Mike shares how many days he's been sober in his sex addiction, his twelve-step meeting plan, and anything else around his sobriety plan.

These check-ins set us up for success. They provide a neutral ground for us to discuss whatever may be going on. We're able to set aside feelings of defensiveness and listen from a supportive, loving place. Doing them has helped us be in real time more than we ever thought we were capable of.

Final Thoughts

Communicating appropriately and consistently is SO hard. It's so easy to get lost in trying to persuade your partner to see something the way you do. Or even to try to manipulate a situation enough to get your partner to admit his ineptitude, or better yet, get her to praise you for your superior ability to always be fair and just (eye roll). Communicating with your partner should be a verbal dance through the highs and lows, flowing with one another while you perform the verbal version of the waltz or salsa. While one gives, the other takes, and vice versa.

With that being said, no relationship can have great communication without each of you being able to effectively listen. Admittedly, it's a struggle, but we try to remind ourselves to listen with the intention of understanding and NOT with the intention of replying. To finish this chapter off, we want to leave you with some food for thought as you transition into the next chapter's topic: "God gave us mouths that close and ears that don't . . . that must tell us something."

5 Listen Up

Jana

I'm so proud of my husband. Let me brag on him for a second. Mike started playing football at age twelve. Just thinking of a young Michael makes me smile—picturing him out there with his oversized pads running into other little dudes. Okay, back to the story. He played all through middle and high school, and when I asked him right now whether he had been captain, he said, "Of course."

Here's where it gets really good. When Mike was in high school he wasn't the star and the best, but he worked his ass off and people respected him and how he treated others. That carried over into his college years. He was a walk-on at James Madison

University. Not a full ride, a walk-on. I emphasize that because it shows how hard my husband worked. He then went from being a college walk-on to playing five years in the NFL. Do you know how unheard-of that is? Mike's odds of making it into the NFL were 0.09 percent.

You might be wondering how this has anything to do with listening, so now I'll get to my point. I remember quite a few times when Mike was down and out about his career after he retired, and he would express that to me. He would say, "I wish I would have played longer, or better, or made more of an impact." I'm embarrassed to admit that I don't think I once told him how sorry I was that he felt that way. I think, correction, I KNOW I would say, "But OMG, babe, look how amazing your career was; you were a walk-on who made it in the NFL and played five years!" I never understood why he would walk away still feeling defeated. I know now, though. I wasn't listening.

"Are You Listening to Me?"

At some point, we have all asked our partners, or our partners have asked us, this question: "Are you listening to me?" The question to ask yourself is, are you *actually listening* to your partner? Or are you just *hearing* while you wait for your chance to respond? There is "listening to understand" and "listening to respond," and the former is what we should all strive for. A 2003 study showed that people who listen to understand feel greater satisfaction in their relationships with other people.

Many people *think* they are listening to understand, but in fact they are merely waiting to respond. You might be able to tell this is happening because your partner gives impersonal, generic responses just to move the conversation along. Or she might seem desperate to talk and isn't making eye contact with you. Maybe your partner isn't listening because he doesn't want to hear what you're going to say, doesn't want to hear the truth spoken out loud.

It can be hard to really listen. Maybe you're someone who listens to understand and takes on all the problems of your friends and family so much that they become your own; eventually, you get to a point where you can't listen anymore because you've completely disregarded your own needs. Or maybe you're just outright exhausted working all day or the kids have worn you out, so the last thing you want to do is listen to someone else's problems or complaints.

All of these might be true, but you need to ask yourself, Are you actually listening? How can you be a more efficient listener?—especially for the person who matters most in your life, your partner.

Active Listening

Active listening is listening to understand, and, if practiced and mastered, it's the best gift you can give to your partner. And to yourself. If done correctly it will supply you with the information you need to be the support you want to be for the one you love. Active listening also involves paying attention to body language—

yours and your partner's. Cueing in to body language can help you identify what feelings come up for you and help you figure out what your partner is feeling if he or she isn't able to articulate it clearly.

Active listening is easy to talk about but damn hard to do. It's hard to do even when you're listening to someone talk about her day or what happened at work. But when she talks about her feelings or about the relationship or about you? How do you not take it personally when your partner starts sharing a negative feeling or experience based on something you did or didn't do to make him feel that way? We know from our own experience that sometimes we hear things differently in those situations.

Mike

When I think about listening, I think about fighting. So often I've cut Jana off or talked over her for fear she was going say the thing that I'm most afraid to hear: "You're not good enough." If Jana shares a feeling of not being supported, for example, I receive that as "I'm not a supportive husband, I've never been, I'm the worst." When I allow my feelings around what she expresses to go to that place, well, I stop listening. Which just validates her feelings of not being supported. So instead of being a rock for her and allowing her to share how she feels about a specific (not generalized) situation and learning more about her, I go to a place where I'm only listening to respond.

If your first words or actions after your partner speaks include "Yeah, but . . . " or "That's bullshit" or an eye roll or a sarcastic "Ohh-kayyy" or "How could you feel that way?" then chances are you're locked and loaded ready to defend and listening only to respond. Those examples are all things I'm guilty of saying or doing, and I bet I'm not alone here.

When Jana expresses a feeling and I start to have those "Yeah, but" responses, sometimes it's because I just don't agree with what she's feeling. In my mind, her feelings don't make rational sense. So if they don't make sense to me, then how could she possibly feel that way?

Well, when it comes down to it, it flat-out doesn't matter whether they make sense to me or not. We can't dictate how another person feels in a given scenario. If Jana doesn't feel supported, then I need to listen to understand so I can figure out why. It doesn't mean that I have to agree with the way she feels or even like it, but I can try to figure out why she feels that way.

You Always . . .

We both understand that it can be challenging to not personalize or generalize another person's feelings that are directed toward us. It takes consistent and conscious effort to get better at staying grounded in those moments. We've learned through our work with therapists that it's not solely on the recipient of feelings to depersonalize or degeneralize what is expressed. Often, people tend to say generalized things like "you always . . . " or "you never . . . " when they are sharing with a partner how they feel. We admit that we're guilty of doing that a lot in the past, leading to some big issues that we've spent many therapy sessions hashing out.

When you're expressing a feeling, it's vital to stay away from "always" and "never." In heated, animated, or irrational moments, it actually might feel like "always" and "never" are accurate: your partner always does this or never does that. When your partner hears those terms, whether he consciously acknowledges their use or not, the words will sit with him and definitely come back around, most likely with a passive, "Well, you said I 'never' ____, so I might as well not do it."

Even just writing about this is messy. This kind of back and forth becomes a childish game that is a never-ending shit show if someone doesn't break the cycle. And "someone" here means both people. If you really want to make the relationship last, then it's going to take effort from both of you. We have to constantly remind ourselves that it's not about "me," it's about "we." It's about the relationship. It's about being willing to be a loving partner and a good person to the one you love. It's about another opportunity to learn more about that person you're sharing your life with—spouse, girlfriend, boyfriend, or someone you're just starting to date. It doesn't matter what stage the relationship is in—it's an opportunity across the board. It should also go without saying that the sooner you realize this, the more successful that relationship can ultimately become.

Tools in Your Relational Toolbox

Listening can be the universal tool in your relational toolbox—or better yet, your study guide for other areas. Think of some of the chapters in this book so far: baggage, triggers, communication. You can improve yourself in all those areas by becoming a better and more efficient listener—through active listening, that is, listening to understand. Being able to hear your partner's pain when she is talking about past baggage will help you be more empathetic because you'll have a better understanding of her. Knowing in more detail what triggers your partner will allow you to avoid potential arguments or hurt feelings by gracefully navigating around them. And last, communicating could become easier because you have practiced the art of listening to understand your partner. With a better overall understanding of what makes that person tick, what she cares about, what worries him and so on, you could greatly strengthen your ability to communicate effectively.

Any area in your relationship can be better through active and intentional listening. Having said all that, let's look at some listening tools that we *try*, keyword TRY, to use regularly.

Change Your Mindset

The first is that you have to change your mindset when you're the one who needs to listen. It all comes down to reminding yourself that it isn't about you, it's about your partner. When you are in the listener's chair, remind yourself, "It's not about me, it's not about me, I'm here for him/her." This will help you get to and stay in an empathetic frame of mind.

Just remember that the feelings you may be pushing aside at the moment while you are listening are not unimportant. They are very important, and there will be a time and a place for you to bring them up with your partner. But that time is not in the moment when she is sharing. It may not even be after he is done. It could be hours later or a day or more later. It's not healthy to push feelings down, but that isn't what you're doing here. You are setting them aside so that your partner can feel heard. You'll have your turn, don't worry.

Eye Contact

Eye contact is imperative when the sharing involves something of a sensitive, negative, or emotional nature. It may seem like an elementary concept, but it's surprisingly difficult to do at times. Regardless of the discomfort that may come along with it, especially if it involves something you don't want to hear, it can be extremely settling for the person sharing feelings if he or she sees you listening intently by looking intently. Second to this is body language, which isn't effective unless you are looking at someone. We both work consciously to make sure that we lean into the other person, sit facing them while making solid yet soft eye contact, avoiding natural habits like crossing arms or slouching in our seat, and even touching that person softly if it's appropriate to do so.

Put Yourself in His/Her Shoes . . .

"How would you feel if you were in my shoes?" We can imagine some eye rolls and sighs right now as you read that overused question. But it's an effective one and has helped us with our listening.

So imagine you want to express some feelings toward your partner that have been eating away at you. Maybe he's been doing something that you haven't mentioned yet, or maybe she hasn't done something that you asked her to do, or in a case like our relationship, maybe it's a past feeling that randomly has come up because of an emotional trigger. So you approach your partner and start to talk, and he immediately starts to defend, cut you off, disregard, or minimize your feelings or even take what you said and turn it around by expressing feelings he has toward you (aka finger-pointing.) How does that make you feel? Pretty shitty and not heard, right?

Now let's go back to the beginning, but this time your partner sits quietly and listens while you express your feelings. Immediately, you feel a little better, don't you? Now let's go back to eye contact for a minute. Your partner is quiet and not defensive, but she isn't looking at you. She's doing something else or is staring out the window while you talk. Do you still feel heard? Probably not, and you'll most likely ask the question we started this chapter with, "Are you listening to me?" Even thinking about this doesn't feel good.

So let's continue with the same scenario, but now your partner is locked in on your eyes and is leaning in toward you. Immediately, you feel more heard. Now just imagine being in close proximity and your partner softly places his hand on your shoulder, back, hand, or leg. Probably a game-changer, right? Well, in our experience, it has been. We can feel the difference in the room; we feel the connectedness of trying to work through the issue at hand. We feel like a team, we feel like partners.

Take a minute to sit with what you've just read. We'll bet some recent scenarios pop up in your head that are similar to this one. Take inventory on what you feel in both situations. If your partner takes the negative path in similar situations, how do you feel? We know the answer here because we get it and have lived and still live through it at times. So as you play these scenarios out in your mind, get honest with yourself: Have you reacted negatively to your partner? Maybe you're more guilty than your partner is? Now you know what it may feel like to be in his/her shoes during those conflicts.

It's kind of annoying that the thing we've heard so many times from parents, teachers, and other adults—"put yourself in the other person's shoes"—has become a tool that we are advocating here. It's even more ironic that it works. It has helped us, and it can help you. Put down the swords and shields in your relationship, open your hearts, be empathetic to your loved one's feelings, and listening can become one of the biggest ways that your relationship's potential can be maximized.

Listening for Praise

This chapter has mostly been about listening to or expressing negative feelings, but that's not always the case. Sometimes someone compliments you, and you should listen to that, too. Some of us quickly push aside, disregard, or undermine compliments; we don't really hear them or take them in, which doesn't make us great listeners. A classic example of this is a woman responding to "You look beautiful" with "Oh, I don't have any makeup on, and my hair's a mess." Or a man's buddy telling him, "You played great on the golf course today," and his responding with, "No way, man, I played terrible." Such responses completely shut down the person who is right in front of you. No one likes to give compliments to people who then reject those compliments.

How nice would it be for both the person giving the compliment and for YOU to accept that compliment—to say in response, "Wow, thank you very much, that just made my day." What a concept, right?

If you're like us, reading that might have made you cringe because it may be hard for you to accept compliments, and this all may sound very cheesy to you. Both of us have been guilty of this. But we encourage and challenge you to try acceptance next time, and we're right beside you, trying to do the same every day. Notice how it makes you feel when you accept a compliment, or when your partner accepts a compliment from you. See how the conversation shifts when you end with accepting rather than deflecting, and you acknowledge the connection between you. It's an experience with lasting benefits for both of you. The person handing you the compliment feels heard, and you feel good about yourself. In most cases we can all call that a win-win.

We constantly give each other compliments but barely acknowledge each other with a genuine thank you or expression of gratitude after we are complimented. We too often follow up with a minimizing detail in an effort to prove we don't deserve the compliment. So if you're like us and struggle with accepting praise, don't beat yourself up—it's a work in progress for us, too.

Here's a little test, though: *Hey reader, we think you're really awesome for reading this book, and we applaud you for being willing to work on yourself to be a better partner in relationships.* And here's where you say, *Thank you!* :)

A Week of Compliments with Jana and Mike

This has become a daily battle for us. We give each other compliments practically every day, and we minimize, or kindly dismiss them, just as regularly. It can be the most insignificant chore, like emptying the dishwasher or doing a load of laundry, or even making dinner. We will compliment the other who completed said task, which is nice, but not required. Which is why the receiving party will respond with, "Uh, yeah, of course." Or "You don't have to thank me, it had to get done." Very seldom has one of us responded with "Thank you, and you're welcome." It's so silly that we yearn for compliments, but when we get them, we don't accept them. It's a vicious cycle that is amusing and somewhat sad, and yet we're both guilty of doing it.

But wait! There's more! It doesn't end there, unfortunately. It has leaked over into physical compliments—the ones that loved ones, friends, and family members all have dealt with. Like the classic "You look beautiful today" being met with "Oh stop, no I don't—I'm so pale and out of shape and I need a haircut." Oh yeah, we do that to each other too. We know we aren't the only ones out there guilty of this.

But wouldn't it be nice to start accepting compliments thrown our way? When we compliment someone, we encourage that person to hear it and receive it. It becomes frustrating when he or she doesn't. We have started consciously trying to put an end to negating compliments that we give to each other. But we still have those days when we don't want to and we'd rather throw ourselves a pity party instead. Who doesn't love a little self-loathing every once in a while? It's the best time to catch up on all the shows you're behind on. :)

Listening and Responding

Let's transition now to a day-to-day challenge that we all face when sitting in the listener's chair: dealing with feedback, advice, and solutions versus silence and support. This challenge covers all relationships—friends, family, and romantic partners.

When someone close to us leans in and shares a situation of struggle, we often feel obligated to try to solve that situation. But did that person ask us to? Or were you not actively listening to what she said? We naturally assume that the reason he is sharing with us is because he needs our help to find a solution. In many cases that may be true, but we've realized through our relationship work that that may not be the case at all. So we've started the practice of asking one another whether we want feedback or help finding a solution, and now we're taking that practice outside of our partnership and using it with our friends as well.

Jana

I've always prided myself for being a good listener and giving the best advice to my friends. But I've learned that sometimes friends just want you to LISTEN and not offer feedback. It's easier to make suggestions, like, "You're better off without him," than to just sit and feel your friends' pain and empathize with it. You may think you're helping them by offering solutions or saying, "It's okay," but in fact, that's just dismissing how they feel. Such comments may even cause them to feel rushed in their feelings.

I don't think I learned that until my relationship with Mike. Wait, what am I saying? I KNOW I didn't learn that until my relationship with Mike. And honestly, I started to go back and feel bad about those previous interactions. So many times I have thought, *Man, I'd like to be able to do that over.* For instance, the conversation regarding Mike and his feelings toward his unfulfilling career in the NFL. I can now imagine what it could have done for him if I'd been able to just sit there and *listen* to what he had to say. Or had enough empathy to say, "I'm so sorry you feel that way," and let that be that. Too often, we're uncomfortable with "letting that be that"; instead, we have to make ourselves feel better and say, "But you made it to the NFL!"

When I respond by trying to offer advice, I'm not being a bad friend or bad wife, but I'm not listening in the way that I should be. I should empathize with my friend and then, as I've learned from my relationship with Mike, ask, "Hey, do want my opinion, or do you just want me to listen?" It's amazing how much deeper my relationships and conversations are now through using this one simple tool.

Now, for sure, just listening can be a lot harder than offering advice—particularly with your spouse, because your spouse can send you off the rails or get under your skin more than anyone else. I think that's where Mike and I have the most trouble. I love to talk to him, down to how many Cheerios I had that morning. I enjoy telling him what's going on, who I talked with that day and what we said, and what I'm thinking and feeling. He has learned to practice patient listening, which is a term I just made up. This happens when you honestly can't give one more F but you do because you know how much it means to your spouse. (Thanks, Mike.)

The bottom line: We don't have to have all the answers for those who confide in us. We just have to be physically and emotionally present for them, because ultimately, that's all they're asking of us. That's what Mike and I ask of each other in our relationship these days. We're both doing a pretty good job at prefacing what we're about to say with, "Hey babe, I just need you to listen to me right now" or "Hey, I need your help with something and would like to talk it out with you." Or if we're the listener, "Before we dive deeper into this topic, do you need me to just listen? Or do you want my feedback?" These suggestions may seem like they're straight out of a textbook or a therapist's mouth, but we promise you, they will help both sides by taking away the power of assumption and helping you be clear about your expectations.

I want to mention one other thing about listening that maybe doesn't happen as much in romantic relationships because you do most things together. But how many times has a friend told you, for instance, about a great trip she took with her kids to the San Diego Zoo, and you immediately responded with, "Well, we just got back from South Africa, and let me tell you, it was amazing!" Did you even acknowledge what your friend said? Or did you just one-up her?

One-upping is a trap for many, us included. You want to share in your friend's excitement, but you do it by relating *your* great experience and excitement. Your friend's San Diego Zoo story pales in comparison to your safari, and she feels one-upped and her experience with her kids feels diminished. Don't feel like you can't share your experiences with your friends, but no one likes a one-upper.

We could keep going down the listening rabbit hole and paint more scenarios, but you get the idea. Here are our general rules for listening:

1. Listen intently.

2. Make and keep eye contact.

3. Have inviting body language.

4. Know that it isn't about you.

5. Empathize.

6. Ask the speaker what he or she needs from you.

At the end of the day, of course, you won't be a perfect listener. It takes a lot of practice, but by using our tools, we've been getting better. You can, too. You're reading this book for a reason, and you're already one step ahead of other people by wanting to grow, learn to fight The Good Fight, and be a better version of yourself. So listen up and keep at it!

6 Tell the Truth

Mike

Those of you who listen to our podcast, *Whine Down with Jana Kramer and Michael Caussin*, might remember back in January 2020 when Jana held things down by doing a "Mom-uary." I wasn't part of the show for a month, and there were a lot of rumors that we had split. Well, let me finally tell you that story.

For about two months I had a Twitter account that Jana didn't know about. Not only did I have a secret, but I was breaking a boundary we had set in our relationship (we'll talk about boundaries later in this chapter). Along with that, I had deleted some text messages between me and a female family friend—someone I had known my whole life. For some relationships, all this may not seem like a big deal. Twitter? A family friend? Nothing to write home about. But for our relationship, this was on the verge of being the final iceberg that sank our ship.

Triggers for Jana aren't just about the context of what happened; her trauma mostly lies in the act of discovery. Having to discover on her own any sort of broken boundary takes her back to the time when she initially discovered my affairs and infidelity. So even though this time I wasn't cheating or sexually acting out in any way, she was still set off because of the earlier trauma I had created in our marriage.

Some of you may be thinking, "Mike, why not just tell the truth, or tell her about the account, or tell her you're texting with your friend? If it's not a big deal, then why hide it from her?" And trust me, I ask myself the same thing. I'll fill you in on my crazy logic later in the chapter, but first, we want to talk about a few concepts we've learned over the years.

Would He/She Be Bothered by This?

Think about a conversation you've recently had with someone (other than your partner), or even a text message exchange—an interaction with a co-worker or a friendly conversation with the person in line in front of you at the grocery store. Got one in mind? Now, ask yourself, and be honest: If your partner were right there next to you during that interaction or conversation, would he or she be bothered by it? Do you get a little jolt of anxiety just thinking about your partner being next to you in that moment?

This is something therapists have asked us. Our immediate, and naturally defensive, reaction is typically, "No, of course it wouldn't bother him/her! I even wish he/she had been there with me. Blah blah blah." But then they encouraged us to pause and really think about it. Was there a time you were a bit too friendly with someone? Or even a bit flirty? Would your partner *really* have no issue with you talking to that very attractive and friendly person in line in front of you? Or texting the co-worker/Russian dance partner who looks like he just walked off set from a GQ photo shoot? (Oh, wait . . .) Which brings us to the main question: Would you act, say, or be the same way in that situation if your partner were right next to you?

This is something we try to be way more conscientious about in our daily lives. We both admit that in our pasts we've been guilty of being flirts. But we want to do better at respecting one another the best ways that we can at all times. And we wanted to share this because it's a way of keeping ourselves in check. Just having that question in mind, "Would this still be okay if he/she were next to me?" does that. So maybe ask yourselves the same question. We'd hate you to fall victim to the pitfall that is justification. More on that later.

This brings up another concept/mantra we learned from one of our masterful therapists: "You're only as sick as your secrets." It's pretty much as simple as that. If you're someone who has held on to or even currently is hanging on to a big secret, then you realize how difficult it is to live day-to-day with that secret. You tend to be more defensive, more on edge, and just miserable. The secret deteriorates your soul as you continue to push people away because of the weight you're carrying every single day.

So how can someone with a secret that is detrimental to themselves or the ones around them live a healthy or peaceful life? We don't have the answer to that, but in our experience, the secret always comes out—either by getting discovered or being disclosed. So remember, if you're holding on to a secret, give yourself the gift of letting it go and getting it out there. You deserve that freedom.

We speak from experience because we have clearly been on both ends of handling the discovery or disclosure of secrets. It's painful to process, yes, but not as painful as holding on to the secret. The unfortunate thing is that secrets can be discovered so often that you can become accustomed to them. Not the pain of them, but the act of their being discovered—almost like you're anticipating when the next bomb is going to drop.

Jana

So, when *is* the next bomb going to drop? That's been a constant question for me throughout the past five years of our marriage. It's been exhausting. I could fill an entire suitcase with "I'll never do it again," "There are no more lies," "I'll never give you another reason to leave." I've learned through therapy why Mike lies to protect himself, and where it comes from, but it doesn't make it any easier to understand at times.

In the past I would think back and wonder how he could have done the things he did and then come home and lie about them—or be so good at lying about them. Thinking about it makes me sick to my stomach, and there are a lot of pictures I can't even look at anymore because it's so painful to be reminded of what his addiction was doing to him, and to us, at that time. Though Mike hasn't cheated with another woman in the past four years, he still has some addictive behaviors around lying and justifying. I can see how an addict who is not in healthy recovery would say defensively, "Well, I'm not sleeping with someone else *now*."

Here's what an addict doesn't get, though: it's not about the *act*, it's about the *lie*. And it's about the *discovery* of the lie. That is what is so damn harmful. That is what makes for an unhealthy downward spiral. Mike and I even had a twenty-four-hour rule: he had twenty-four hours to correct his lie. If he did that, he would be showing growth and change, and also I wouldn't be so afraid that I would discover something. One of our therapists told us that affairs don't usually cause divorce; lies do.

I learned something in therapy that has been really helpful for me at times. I would think that because Mike was lying, it meant that he didn't choose me, that he didn't love me, that he must have NO empathy for what he put me through, and he must be lying about everything. My mind spirals there, so I go straight to "I can't do this anymore." But therapy helped me distinguish between *hurt* and *harm*. Mike is going to hurt me again; he will make me cry, we will fight again in unhealthy ways, and we may hurt each other again with words. But what *harms* me? In our marriage, harm for me would be discovering more lies and secrets.

So when we have a fight, instead of going to "I can't do this anymore" and calling a girlfriend for the hundredth time and telling her I'm going to file for divorce, I'm going to do something different. I'm going to take a beat. I'm going to sit with my feelings. I'm going to differentiate between hurt and harm and gather all the facts that I know to be true before acting out a scene from *The Young and the Restless*.

Rebuilding Brick by Brick

"How do I repair trust?" "Can I ever trust again?" These are two of our most common internet searches. Want to guess what the underlying theme to all the answers is? Yahtzee!—you guessed it: time. But that doesn't really explain how to repair trust. We get it: "Time heals all wounds." But time doesn't do the work for you. That's up to you and your partner.

Trust is the hardest thing to get back in any relationship. If trust is broken, it's a long road back to redemption. We've had to learn to accept that. We both want to rush the process at times. We both want to hurry up and feel trusted, or hurry up and be able to trust. Unfortunately, as we all know, it doesn't work that way. Our couples therapist suggested that we look at this from a more "micro" viewpoint rather than looking at the big picture. He used the analogy of building a house: brick by brick. It's the same for our relationship. No single act is going to magically instill trust in the relationship; it's one day at a time, one brick at a time.

This was difficult for us to accept at the beginning because we wanted a trustworthy act to count for more, when in reality, it was just *one* brick of many. We were drowning in distrust, so anytime something good happened, we wanted to take it for more than it was. Eventually, we were able to get the hang of taking each brick for what it was and stacking them up one by one. Our challenge has been the fact that things have happened that continue to knock the wall down. Having to rebuild such a delicate wall is a painful and exhausting process. But as we continue to build, we can feel its strength grow the more bricks we add to it.

A brick can be many things. It could be saying you're going do something and following through with it, or it could be leaning into your partner with feelings and vulnerability. Anything that shows a change in behavior, integrity, or respect can build more bricks.

Most of the work in this situation is up to the person who did something to injure trust in the relationship—the person we previously called the "perpetrator." It's that person's job to show up and do things that help build bricks. The main job of the "victim" is to observe. It's also helpful for the victim not to shame the perpetrator and constantly remind him or her of the actions that caused the situation. Those moments are inevitable, but doing your best to stay away from that will help the rebuilding and healing happen faster.

Jana

"Do you trust Mike?" This is the number one question I get in my Instagram direct messages every day. The answer is, "Yes, today I do." Today I see him working his program, I see him showing up as a father and a husband, and I see his words matching his actions. How he is showing up looks different than before, which helps me trust him. And, as we've said, it takes time to see that change. Give yourself the grace and patience while you continue to rebuild.

My therapist also taught me that staying present (see Chapter 11) is the best way to sustain trust. If I start rehashing the past or worrying about the future, I can easily send my thoughts down a dark path. The past is just as it is—the past. And we can't do anything about it now. We can't go back, we can't change it, and it will always be there. How, or whether, you let the past dictate how you feel today, though, is up to you and you alone. It can sometimes be easy to live in the past because you and Lonely are friends, but it's a bad place to live when you're wanting to fight. And like any Good Fight, the two of you both need to stay present in order to see the change and growth.

Quick Note from Jana

You might think that trust is only a one-sided deal if you're the one who got hurt . . . like I did. Well, wrong. Your spouse also needs to feel safe and believe he or she can trust you. To which you might say (like I did), "Well, I've done nothing wrong." Sure. AND (as our therapists like to say) there is also another side to this. I have shamed Mike back and forth a few football fields with the nasty comments I've thrown at him since discovery. Were they valid and true? Some. But there comes a point when you have to stop screaming from a rooftop because over time your partner may stop trusting you and ultimately may leave the relationship. Because growth needs to happen on both sides.

How can your partner trust you with a feeling or thought he might have if you're just going to shame him? How can she come to you if she fears your reaction? Invite your partner to come to you and validate her with a "thank you for sharing." He will start to trust you more if your reaction isn't so heightened and he can feel like he can talk to you as a friend.

Mike

People ask me, "Why don't you just tell the truth? How hard is that?" And I ask myself that same damn question. I wish it were easy for me; I wish it were simple and black and white. I'd like to think that I'm not alone when it comes to this level of difficulty with something that seems so simple. But let me give you a little backstory to help those who may not understand where I'm coming from.

I started lying at a young age. It was a habit I picked up as a protective mechanism, and it often proved to be an efficient tool. Unfortunately, the people I was trying to protect myself from were my parents. They are extremely morally sound people and put a ton of emphasis on the importance of being honest—making it ironic that lying ultimately became my biggest character defect. Regardless of their emphasizing such an important character trait, I still developed the bad habit—all because I learned to fear the truth because of experiences in my life. I was a very sensitive child, and I hated upsetting my parents. So as my brain started to develop, I learned more coping mechanisms in order to protect myself. I learned different ways of lying. It became less and less black and white for me.

Through all the therapy I've done over the years, I've been able to answer the questions of why, how, and when regarding my lying. I admit that even when I began to come to these realizations, I wanted to blame my parents. I started saying things like, "Well, if they hadn't been so hard on me . . ." or "Maybe if they had showed me more grace in situations . . ." or "They shouldn't have *made* me feel. . . ." That's where, with more work, I was able to finally stop myself and realize that no one *made* me feel any particular way.

Sure, we can all feel certain ways because of the actions of people around us, but no one *makes* us feel a particular feeling.

As a kid you don't have the ability to come to that realization, so of course you blame your parents—just like when you got grounded as a kid but still blamed your parents for it. *You* got yourself in that situation, not your parents. My point here is that I'm able to look back and realize that my parents did the best they could and are still doing the best they can. Especially now that I'm a parent myself, I can really respect and appreciate the job they did with me and my siblings. I had an amazing childhood and wouldn't trade it for another.

My parents and I have talked a lot about things over the past few years as I've grown as a person, a man, and a husband. They expressed their fears or concerns that what has happened between me and Jana because of my addiction and lies was possibly their fault. But I told them this: My experience as a kid was my experience and no one else's. I processed information, reacted the way I did, handled feelings the way I did all because that is how I survived, and simply put, it's just how I did it—period. Another kid in the same situations would probably process, react, and handle their emotions in a completely different way. We're all different, regardless of the similarities we might share in our experiences.

Have I learned what *not* to do as a parent in some situations based on how I was raised? Absolutely—we all do that. My parents learned from their parents, your parents learned from theirs, and we all try to mimic the positives and change the negatives. It happens in every single family and will continue to happen for generations.

The Lies We Face

We all lie. We're sure you've all heard of or made the kinds of lies we list here. But have you actually considered them lies in the past? Or are you *justifying* leaving out some information or *minimizing* some aspects of a story to decrease its potential impact? Defining these types of lies helps to shed light on them so we can all be more conscious of them every day. Because of Mike's extensive history of lying to the people closest to him, we want to make sure to acknowledge all the different masks that a lie can wear.

ERROR—a lie made by mistake. People believe they're being truthful, but what they're saying isn't true.

OMISSION—leaving out relevant information. This kind of lie is easy and least risky, and it is mostly used as a protective mechanism. It's a passive deception, so liars often feel less guilty.

JUSTIFICATION—defending the context or intention of a lie, validating it with the big picture and looking past the act of lying itself.

DENIAL—refusing to acknowledge a truth. Typically, the underlying feeling behind denial is shame. People in denial may be lying to themselves.

MINIMIZATION—reducing the effects of a lie.

EXAGGERATION—representing something or someone as greater, better, more experienced, or more successful.

FABRICATION—deliberately inventing a false story (aka making shit up).

Keep these kinds of lies in mind moving forward. We try to use these definitions as ways to call ourselves out and lean into each other. We might say something like, "When you asked me how much I spent on Amazon (after you saw all those boxes show up at the front door), I later realized that I minimized that because I was afraid of your response. I actually spent $600, not a couple hundred." Sure, you'll probably still upset someone with your lie, but not nearly as much as if you hadn't corrected the minimization (aka the lie) and that person found out about it later.

This brings us to one of the biggest tools we're using more than ever right now.

Boundaries

Early in our marriage recovery, the concept of boundaries was a difficult one to get on the same page about, so it's been a point of contention. Now, thankfully, we're both on the same side of this and respect what boundaries do for our marriage and what they give us in the form of trust and transparency. Boundaries are important, but they can be tricky to navigate, so we're going to share our own personal boundaries in our marriage to give those of you who don't know much about boundaries an idea of what they look like and how they can work in a relationship.

Boundaries are so much more than "rules" of the marriage or lists of what a person can or can't do or isn't "allowed" to do in a relationship. They are about understanding who you are, who your partner is, what both of your needs are, and how to respect those needs. You want each other to feel comfortable in your relationship and to be able to develop positive self-esteem within it.

And it's always important to remember that boundaries have NOTHING to do with control over one another. The motivation behind them should be based solely on developing and nurturing a sense of personal safety in your relationship.

In order to establish boundaries, you need to be clear with your partner about

- who you are,

- what you want,

- what you believe and value,

- and what your limits are.

Don't think anything is off-limits here. If you think it, feel it, or believe it, then speak on it. We understand that it can be nerve-wracking because you may fear that something you say could scare off your new partner. That's understandable, but it's a risk you need to take. Otherwise, you're compromising yourself and your self-worth in order to please or avoid displeasing someone else.

We saw a good example of this during a TV interview of Anna Kendrick. The question was along the lines of, "What was craziest reason for why you ended a relationship?" Her answer was that he wouldn't stop tickling her. We looked at each other and chuckled. The interviewer did the same and then asked her to explain. She said that early in their relationship she told this man that she didn't like to be tickled. But he kept tickling her, thinking it was a joke. After reminding him numerous times, she finally broke up with him. She had told him that it was a boundary of hers, and he didn't respect it, so it was "Peace out."

This may seem silly, but the point is this: regardless of what your partner may think of your boundary, it is still YOUR boundary, not his or hers. It is your partner's choice whether to respect it or not.

We want to share some of the boundaries we've set in our relationship. Of course, they're specific to us, but they can give you an idea of what can count as a boundary and how they can work.

ONE-ON-ONES (WITH THE OPPOSITE SEX): We don't see any reason to have a one-on-one lunch, dinner, coffee, or meeting of any kind with someone of the opposite sex. If it has to do with work, then you can always find someone to include as a third party who still has a purpose for being there. Even if it is with our spouse's best friend, the question still remains: What reason is there to be in that situation? Granted, unforeseeable and unavoidable circumstances can arise. We aren't saying that a one-on-one will never happen. We just don't plan them or put ourselves in any kind of situation like that when possible.

DELETING AND HIDING MESSAGES: We all delete spam and unimportant and pointless emails. Our point with this boundary is based on intention. If one of us is deleting our call log, search history, text messages, or emails in order to keep something from the other, then that is definitely ignoring a boundary. But intent is important: if we delete the confirmation email of a gift we just got for the other, then that is obviously fine.

CHEATING/LYING: We wouldn't be off-base calling cheating and lying deal-breakers. We're sure that most of you feel the same way. Lying and transparency are related, but the difference for us is that lying is more black and white. You either lied or you didn't. Transparency can live in a gray area; maybe you didn't lie, but some information you gave wasn't entirely accurate. It could have been purposely or even accidentally skewed in some way.

Related to this boundary is rigorous honesty. "Rigorous" means, severely exact or accurate. That's how we strive to be with one another in every way we can. We strive to correct any inaccuracy or lie in a situation if we weren't initially completely upfront. So we might come back with, "Hey, I know earlier when you asked me about __, I said __. In reality, it was __." We've done well with this, and it's important that the person receiving this level of honesty doesn't react negatively.

NAME-CALLING: Name-calling during an argument has no place in our marriage. We didn't do this early in our relationship, but now we strictly stand by it.

PHYSICAL VIOLENCE: This definitely has zero place in our relationship.

SLAMMING DOORS: This is something we did early on, too, but now we make sure we never leave a room this way.

RESPECT FOR PRIVACY: This is a two-parter. First, we feel that when we get in an argument, running off and "venting" to other people isn't the thing to do. We keep our day-to-day business close to the chest and within our small circle of closest friends whom we trust. Second, no snooping. The act of snooping is stressful FOR BOTH PARTIES. That often goes unsaid. Feeling like your partner is trying to catch you doing something feels awful, especially when you're being rigorously honest and transparent. Meanwhile, feeling like your partner may be doing something behind your back also blows. Respecting privacy but being willing to share proof of that transparency when prompted is how we keep the stress to a minimum and respect each other through the process. So if one of us is feeling uneasy or triggered, then we can ask the other, for instance, whether we can look at their phone.

Again, this list is specific to us. And it's specific for now; boundaries can vary over time. Needs change as relationships change. It's okay to add boundaries as you need them, BUT it's not just something you can spring on your partner randomly or out of insecurity. You need to have a sit-down conversation around them so you can both explore why a boundary might be needed.

Quick Note from Mike

Just to be transparent with y'all, we have boundaries that are specific to situations as well. Situational boundaries aren't meant to last forever but to help create trust and protect the relationship during a sensitive time.

Going to bars is a situational boundary for us. I haven't gone to a bar with friends, co-workers, or anyone else for a while. And this boundary hasn't been easy for me to respect. When Jana expressed this as a boundary, I got extremely defensive because to me it felt like she was trying to control me. But I'm sure the women reading this—and even the men if they imagine the roles reversed—can see why at a highly sensitive time in a relationship, bars aren't the best place to imagine your partner being. Drinking and hanging with single people, especially if you have a family, can seem like an unnecessary indulgence in time and energy. It took some time and therapy to get past my issues around this, but eventually I was able to get to the place where I realized it wasn't about Jana trying to control me. It was about her needing to feel safe. And that is all I want for her: I want her to feel safe, loved, and secure at all times.

But inevitably a friend will ask, "Hey Mike, want to have a few drinks tonight?" Maybe this is a new friend, maybe it's someone I'd rather meet for coffee because I know how he is when he drinks, or maybe this is a longtime friend who I know might be itching for a night on the town. The question is, "Is a night on the town tonight going to be good for *my* family? Or is this a time when I should try to show up for a friend who may be going through a difficult time?" And that's where situational boundaries are helpful. They are boundaries that are more about conversations and sharing, bringing Jana in and our coming to a decision together.

Consequences

Boundaries are similar to Newton's third law: *For every action, there is an equal and opposite reaction*. Their equal and opposite reaction would be considered consequences. Consequences tend to have a negative connotation, but there are positive consequences too. When we respect each other's boundaries, we both feel safer, more connected, more loved and appreciated. You just can't put a price on that when talking about a relationship. The flip side to that are the negative consequences that occur if a boundary isn't respected or followed.

The emotional consequences that occur on the negative side could simply be the opposite to the positive consequences. Instead of feeling safer, you feel less safe; instead of more connected, less connected, and so on. In addition, there can and should be situational/physical consequences when boundaries are broken. Here are a few examples:

- End of relationship/marriage

- Sleep in another room

- No sex

- Alone time/space (could be twenty minutes, could be a few hours)

- Period of separation (such as going away for the weekend)

These kinds of consequences should match the "offense." For example, we aren't going to end our marriage because one of us slammed a door, but we may ask for some space or even for the person who slammed the door to sleep in another room that night.

Consequences can sometimes register as punishment, but with an important difference: consequences have been agreed on beforehand. Both of us know that if one of us slams a door, we're not sleeping together that night. This is a necessary action we implement in order to help us process and feel safe, and we don't need to have the passive-aggressive conversation in order to implement it. This consequence is understood and accepted.

Consequences can also be specific to situations. Let's say your partner has been drinking a lot, and it has gotten out of hand. You've asked him or her to slow down or stop completely, but still no luck. So instead, you start setting specific boundaries around it, such as:

- No going to bars

- No sleeping in the same bed after drinking

- No sex after any amount of drinking

- No buying or keeping alcohol in the house

- No lying or covering up for the drinker if he or she does something stupid while drinking

- No riding with the drinker in the car or allowing the kids to do so

Again, setting boundaries like these has nothing to do with trying to control or punish the other person. They are simple requests in order for you to feel safe around a specific situation. And although some boundaries can seem totally crazy later when you head into a conversation, we encourage you to still set them. You'll be surprised what kinds of realizations can come from simply talking about the worst-case scenario, and also how badly you'll wish you had made a plan for the worst if the worst happens.

So regardless of the interworkings of your relationship, we still strongly encourage you to sit down with your partner and have an open discussion about boundaries. This can really dilute any jealous, resentful, or pent-up negative feelings.

Food for Thought

When going over boundaries one session with our couples therapist, he asked us whether we wanted to get an A or a C grade in our relational boundaries. We looked at him somewhat perplexed, but both of us responded without hesitation, "An A." In response, he left us with this: "If you look at your boundary list, and your intention is to just check the box and do exactly what it says on that list, then you're limiting yourselves, and that would be getting a C. But if you focus on not just staying within the boundaries but on living with the highest integrity at all times, then hopefully you won't come close to breaking those boundaries.

The way we see it, if you shoot for a C, the highest grade you'll get is a C. But if you shoot for an A, and the worst you do ends up being a C, which is still living by all the boundaries, well, then the relationship is in good shape.

7 Learn to Walk Away

"Hey Mike, did you take care of _____ yet?"

"*No, not yet, sorry, I will soon.*"

"Okay, when will that be?"

"*I don't know, when I do.*"

"Okay, well, can you get it done soon?"

"*Jana, I told you I will do it. Where's the fire?*"

"You don't have be like that, Mike. I just thought you would have done it by now."

"*Well, you never said 'Do it by Tuesday.' You asked me to do it, and I told you I would take care of it. Why isn't that good enough? Why couldn't you just say 'okay' when I gave you my response and trust that I would get it done?*"

"Here we go . . . I'm not saying you're not good enough, Mike. I just want to know when it's going to get done."

"Why does it matter when it's going to get done? You asked me to do it, and I told you I would, so why don't you just let me?"

"Why are you getting so defensive, Mike? I just asked a question."

"No, you didn't, Jana, it's never just a simple question with you. You always have follow-up questions that include something you want to get off your chest."

"Well, I'm just curious why you haven't done it yet. You didn't have much going on this week, so I figured you would have already done it."

"So because I didn't do it on your timeline, you have an issue around it not being done. Surprise!—things need to be on your timeline, otherwise there's an issue."

"No, Mike, I'm not saying it has to be on my timeline. But if you want to get into this, then yes, I do feel like you procrastinate. And it's frustrating to me because I'm constantly doing a million other things."

"Okay, so now all of a sudden I don't work hard?!"

And scene! Well, that was fun, wasn't it.

Does any of that seem familiar? We're sure it does for some of y'all out there. We stopped the dialogue there because that's the pivotal point where the conversation can go in one of two directions. It can go down the healthy, productive, learn-about-each-other path, or the other path. Unfortunately, that has been a frequent scenario in our household over the past few years, and early on we often took the darker path. It's so frustrating that such a small, seemingly insignificant topic of conversation can create deeper, more triggering feelings during an interaction.

This has been part of our reality and a major part of our work to improve ourselves when it comes to conflict. Too many times, scenarios like this have occurred over stupid, petty issues. But they escalate because of a multitude of reasons ranging from triggers, validated fears, unmet expectations, not feeling heard, not feeling appreciated, feeling attacked, or not feeling like we are enough. Those may all seem different, but actually they are all similar—because they all stem from *feelings*. But in those escalating moments, it's not always easy to identify, let alone talk about, what you're feeling and why. What has helped steer us down the healthy path more frequently during such scenarios has been our growing ability and commitment to walking away.

This is one of those things that is so so so much easier said than done. Once you start gaining that momentum toward an argument in a conversation, it can be a difficult train to stop. One or both of you start to talk a little faster, then you get a little louder, and the next thing you know you're yelling and you don't even remember how you got there. It's obviously not healthy, but we've all been there.

Too many times after these situations we would come back together to apologize, thinking it would feel resolved, when in fact, it didn't. It may feel like it momentarily, but underneath it all are those feelings we were both harboring from the argument. Our growing battle then and still to this day is figuring out those underlying feelings earlier in the conversation.

In this chapter we share with you some of our personal insights, experiences, and helpful tips that we've learned about walking away. Again, as we've already said, we aren't experts and don't claim to be. What we share is based on our own personal experiences. But we hope is that by sharing what we've learned, we can give you some insights to help you in your relationship.

What Lies Beneath

Have y'all ever had those arguments that almost feel like an out-of-body experience? Where it feels like you're on the sideline watching yourself say ridiculous, childish, or even hurtful things to somebody else or your partner? We definitely have, and we hate the helpless feeling that comes along with it. But what is that feeling, and where does it come from?

Mike

I've had that out-of-body feeling countless times. Too many times, frankly, and it isn't great. It's that "what the fuck am I doing?!" feeling, but you can't stop it. It's like that little angelic Mike on my right shoulder is bound and gagged while that little asshole Mike on my left shoulder has taken over the wheel. I'll be saying or doing things that I know are wrong, immature, or even mean. But even when I realize what I'm doing, I can't stop myself.

It wasn't until I started therapy that I began to dive deep into those moments and find out what was actually lying beneath my unhealthy reactions. It wasn't the same thing every time; it would vary, depending on circumstances. At times, it was triggering feelings of not being good enough. Other times, I could feel like my character was being attacked.

This is a big part of the issue in the example above. When Jana said that she thinks I procrastinate a lot, I immediately took it as though she had said I wasn't a hard worker at all. Even though I know that's the farthest thing from the truth, I still have that feeling of needing to defend myself. Not because I think there's truth to it. It's purely because I pride myself so much at being a hard worker, so I take offense if Jana or anyone says otherwise. We all have things like that—perceived pillars of our personality that we can't handle being challenged.

That kind of escalation can also happen when something doesn't make sense to me, so I wonder why we are even discussing it. But regardless of the situation, there's one common denominator: my inability to express what I'm feeling. To go a step further, it was my inability to even *identify* that feeling. My therapist in Los Angeles has helped me be able to change my mindset and begin to assess my feelings and emotions as they arise. I'm still learning and trying to master this; it takes a ton of practice. Here's what he has encouraged me to do when these moments come up:

- Be aware of physical sensations.

- Ask yourself, *What am I feeling?*

- Follow that up with, *Why am I feeling this way?*

The next step is key because it dictates which direction the conflict will go. If you're able to pause the conversation with your partner and express to her in a good way what's coming up for you, that is ideal.

Let's look again at the scenario we started the chapter with— where I said, "I don't know, when I do." This is a perfect example of what I'm talking about. Just rereading that part myself, I feel some physical sensations—such as a tightness in my shoulders, clenched teeth, or my body temperature rising. So instead of responding with that somewhat dismissive, smart-ass comment, I could have noticed those physical sensations and then said something along the lines of, "I'm feeling some tension and anxiety in my body right now, and I don't want it to come out sideways." By paying attention to my physical sensations and any kind of tension that might be in the air, I'm inviting Jana to express how she may *truly* feel so we don't escalate the situation.

Of course, it's not always that simple to identify the feelings beneath what I start to experience physically. Usually, the scenario plays out to the point where we stopped it above, and then I'm faced with the decision: either to allow my emotions to get the better of me, or to take control and express to Jana that some deeper issues are coming up for me and I'd like to take a break so I can figure out what they are. That is, I need to walk away.

This is still a conscious and constant challenge for me. It genuinely frustrates me that I have such difficulty with being able to articulate my emotions from a good place. I'm sick and tired of going off the rails in such situations. In so many other areas of my life, I'm calm, cool, and collected. But for whatever reason, when it comes to conflict in my marriage, I have an incredibly hard time. That is all part of my work as a partner and a husband. And my main motivation isn't even to do it for Jana— it's for myself. I want to learn how to live in peace and not take things so personally.

It has taken me and Jana a lot of time and work to start learning our default reasons for why we become so activated. But this is where walking away has played a big part. It has allowed us additional time to be introspective and sit with the feelings and physical sensations we have in charged moments. Doing so gives us the ability to learn from ourselves about ourselves—all with the end goal of being able to manage uncomfortable situations better as people and as a couple.

What's Your Goal?

When you find yourself in an argument, what lies underneath your frustrations? What is your goal?

1. Do you want to be right?

2. Or do you want to be heard?

We have been asked these questions a lot of times in our individual therapy sessions, and we have both sometimes answered, "Well, both." There's nothing wrong with that, necessarily. That's just how we, and probably you, feel at times. That being said, nothing will be resolved if your goal remains, *I want to be right*.

So when we get stuck in that place, we remind ourselves to look more deeply at those underlying feelings and determine what our end game is. But ultimately, the only direction you can go for any kind of reconciliation is the way of being heard, *not* the way of being right.

This brings up the difference between being *heard* and being *understood*. Oftentimes, we get the two confused, which can be frustrating. Say we take a beat from each other and separate in order to calm down during an argument. We reconvene, thinking things will go smoothly because we walked away. Yet we find things escalating again because one or both of us came back to the situation with the expectation that the other would not only hear our feelings, but understand them. This is an unfair expectation, however, because another person can never comprehend exactly why you may feel the way you do in a situation. That other person has a completely different set of triggers and interpersonal complexities that make up his or her emotional responses.

We continue to work on this by understanding that all we can ask of each other is to be heard and to be empathetic when we share. The other doesn't have to agree or know why, but she or her does need to acknowledge.

Don't You Know Me?

This is a question that holds value and carries some weight in situations of conflict. We've all gotten to the point where we have probably said or done something to our partner in an argument with the sole purpose of pissing them off or even hurting them. Come to think of it, maybe this should be more of a statement: "You know me." If you know me, why would you say or do something to purposely harm me? We know our partners better than anyone else. We trust them with our deepest secrets and most vulnerable information. Yet when we get heated with them, we may want to use or trigger those painful feelings in retaliation.

It's just one of those things to be conscious of. It makes us sad when we've both gotten to that point of wanting to hurt or trigger on purpose. Feelings and emotions can be a bitch to process, handle, and comprehend. But the last thing we want to do is emotionally shank the person we love most in this world. That ultimately creates more triggers and validates fears in your partner. Which leads to more distance between the two of you.

Who, What, How, and Why

It's debatable whether walking away is a positive thing for your relationship or whether it hinders connection. We initially heard both ideologies from our therapists, but once we dove more and more into the process, we decided that walking away was an important tool for us. But it must be used in a healthy way. And it can help to understand the personality of your partner.

Jana

In my past relationships, I was always the person who not only ran from my feelings, but also couldn't sleep until we talked out conflicts. This may seem contradictory, so I'll break it down for you.

I've always hated confrontation, but when it came to relationships, I would want to talk about it till I was blue in the face even if it was approaching 3 a.m. I couldn't eat or sleep until a problem was resolved. Now enter Mike. He tends to walk away more times than not in our relationship, and early on I had a hard time with that. Here's what I learned, though: his walking away doesn't mean that he doesn't care or that he doesn't want to talk to me. It may mean that he needs time to gather his thoughts, or maybe that he's tired because it's late, or now I realize that he just might not be in a healthy space to have the conversation we need to have.

Being in this relationship has helped me start to walk away and take a minute because sometimes that's what's healthiest for the relationship. I've realized that when I walk away and take a beat, I have more time to think about the fight or situation from a cleaner, nonheightened emotional state. Having said all that, though, I still won't get a good night's rest if we don't squash it before night's end. It's just how I'm wired.

There are always compromises somewhere along the way in any marriage or relationship. This was one of those areas where Mike and I had to learn through trial and error. We tried to push through it at times, exhausting ourselves with late nights and repetitive conversations and ultimately battling one another to be heard. Which doesn't work, I might add. Then we started walking away. At the start, we even got that wrong. There were times when we thought leaving the room slamming the door behind us was "walking away," or saying something along the lines of "Fine, I'm leaving" would suffice—both childish and wrong.

We learned that for walking away to work, we had to do it from a better emotional place. Unfortunately, we sometimes used it as a trump card to shut the other person down, when really, it's supposed to be used from an empathetic place, informing your partner that you aren't able to be present in that moment because something is going on with you internally. This isn't about dismissing one another; it's about being as supportive and understanding as you possibly can.

Here's our list for how to walk away during an argument, including examples of how we try to say it in those moments:

- Politely address the fact that you're having a hard time staying present and grounded. ("Sorry to stop you, babe, but some feelings are coming up that are getting in the way of my hearing you the way you need to be heard.")

- Reassure your partner that you want to hear what he has to say. ("I don't want you to think that I'm dismissing your feelings, but I need a few to sort this out.")

- Identify an exact time to come back and pick up where you left off. ("Can I come back to you in thirty minutes and try again?") It's imperative that you come back exactly when you said you were going to. If you find you need more time, communicate that.

- When you come back, ask whether your partner is in a good place to keep talking. If she isn't, respect that and leave her be. She then needs to realize that the ball is now in her court to invite you back to talk.

This all probably sounds so easy and calm, doesn't it? Yeah, not all of our experiences are like that either. But we have had some interactions that have gone exactly like that—usually around less personal or triggering topics, but it can be that calm during the rough ones, too. It all depends on how early you catch the shit brewing inside of you.

So let's jump into a more realistic scenario. You're arguing, shit starts escalating, and before it really turns south, one of you says, "All right, we need to walk away from this right now." We've done enough work and practice with this that now if one of us says this, we understand that it is time to walk away. Mike and I sat down and agreed together that if one of us says this, the other HAS to listen and abide by it.

We experienced situations getting out of hand often enough in our relationship that we knew what would happen if we didn't walk away. We follow strict boundaries when doing this. We both make sure that during the "walk-away" we still respect the relationship. For us, that includes staying within the general boundaries of our relationship and not bitching and moaning to friends. That doesn't mean no venting at all; it just means doing so to that one person who is a safe space—whether it's the friend you trust the most or your therapist. We believe that the walk-away time isn't for bitching; it's a therapeutic period to allow those heightened, uncontrollable feelings to subside so you can better understand what you're feeling and why. We also believe that it's very important not to communicate during walk-away time. Don't open that door or fall into the trap of a texting war. What fight has ever been resolved through texts? So unless something comes up about your kids or something else that's necessary in that moment, try to refrain from speaking.

Keeping these boundaries has been critical in order for us to truly benefit from taking those breaks when needed. Here's another story that will shed some light on a few other points we want to leave you with.

Mike

I physically feel lighter after taking breaks from fighting, which is great evidence to support the ways that walking away can help you. In those moments of irrational emotion, I would get so caught up in making my point that I couldn't imagine that a "break" would help me at all. But nowadays I can feel those physical and emotional weights being lifted. In order for this to work for me, though, I have to remind myself of one thing: don't rush it.

I can't tell you the number of times early on that Jana and I would separate, take that time to calm down, and then start the conversation back up only for me to get retriggered by something she said and go right back into an unhealthy mindset. I did it time after time. For a while, I thought that maybe it just wasn't possible for me to collect myself and have a healthy dialogue. But I finally realized that I wasn't giving myself what I needed. I would convince myself that I was good to go way too soon, only to rush back in and get even more defensive than before.

Ultimately, I realized that I needed to find a way to take more time in those moments apart. So instead of just going to another room, I started leaving the house entirely. But it wasn't just leaving that ended up being the answer for me; it was finding something to occupy my time after I left. So I started going to the movies. That became my thing. I've always been a movie buff, and going to the movie theater is one of my favorite things to do, period. So this became my therapeutic answer, my two- to three-hour getaway. Now, I don't use this as an excuse to just get out of the house and go see a movie. I use it when I need to, and Jana knows the difference.

I have a funny story about that, though. One time, when a fight ended up getting to the place where I needed to walk away, I was like, "Fine, I'm going to the movies, I'll be back in a few hours." I left the house and then realized I still had about an hour until the movie started. I hadn't eaten lunch yet, so I went to McDonald's, drove up to the drive-thru window, and ordered a Big Mac Value Meal, a ten-piece chicken McNuggets, a double cheeseburger (with Mac sauce, obvi), and a large sweet tea. I kid you not; I still remember that order to this day. So as I sat in the movie theater parking lot shamefully stuffing my face with ten thousand calories, I began to feel overwhelmed with sadness. Maybe about the fight with Jana or maybe about the ridiculously unhealthy and embarrassing McDonald's order. For the book's sake, let's say it was the former (when really we all know it was most likely the latter). In any case, I was depressed and sad and so tired of fighting with my wife. I didn't even want to go to the movie anymore. So I turned the keys, started the engine, and drove my ass home to sort everything out.

Jana and I had an amazingly connected discussion when I got home, and it was one of the first that really proved to us the benefit of walking away. So, thank you McDonald's.

Our Theory

This works, people. This is an important way to help you fight The Good Fight. We believe that everyone can benefit from this as we have, because by taking the time to walk away, you're able to have calmer conversations with more connected resolutions. As the famous proverb says, "He who fights and runs away, may live to fight another day." #Cliché. But honestly, it rings very true for us. Why allow an argument to continue to escalate to the point beyond repair? You can't take back words you say. (Trust us, we've tried, and it doesn't work.) We've seen a significant decrease in volatile arguments between us and an increase in our rebound time because of our ability to walk away just a little bit more.

You've probably also heard the "never go to bed angry" theory, right? We understand why and how that can be one way to go. We aren't going tell you not to do it if it works for you. We tried that early in our relationship, and it seemed to work—until it didn't, because we were just pushing down feelings without resolving them in order to not go to bed angry. So then, still following that same theory, we said, "Okay, we're going to resolve this before we go to bed." Well, then we found ourselves forcing the issue, which in turn could escalate things, or we were up till 2:00 in the damn morning figuring it out. Waking up the next morning tired and miserable after not enough sleep didn't help our connection. So we decided that getting a good night's sleep (in separate beds, if need be) was more helpful to resolving an argument and gave us healthier outcomes.

To remind y'all for the hundredth time, this is all drawn from our own opinions and experiences. You can figure out what works best for you when faced with an unmovable object during an argument. But if you decide to add walking away to your toolbox, just remember:

- Address the situation calmly (avoid the "fuck-yous" and slammed doors).

- Communicate when you will be back and follow through.

- Respect the relationship.

- When you do come back, ask whether your partner is ready to talk. If not, then respect his or her space.

The ultimate goal is always to respect one another even when you may feel like enemies. We understand how hard that is, especially because our partners are the ones who have the uncanny ability to annoy us more than anyone else. If all else fails, just remember, "Kill 'em with kindness." ;)

8 Pray on It

Mike

Okay, I'm going to go a level deeper here with y'all. It's not like I haven't done that enough already, but this chapter topic has encouraged me to share something a bit more intimate and personal. Several times on our podcast, *Whine Down*, I've touched on my inability to be intimate, but this involves more than that. Let me share the situation.

Jana and I are settling down for the evening. The kids are in bed and our wineglasses are full as we head into our bedroom. When we first get into bed, we both hop on our laptops to do some more Christmas shopping. We're taking turns showing our screens to one another regarding gift ideas for the kids. When Jana shows me her screen, I just turn my head to look at it from the position

I'm in. But when I show Jana a screen, she puts her computer aside and basically gets cheek to cheek with me to look at it.

I understand she yearns for closeness and physical touch, but in my head, I'm like, "Okay, a liiitttttle too close." But I don't say anything; I just allow her to keep getting in my personal space. But each time I'm getting more and more uncomfortable. Then once we're done spoiling our kids for the night, we take some big "sips" of wine and get into more comfortable positions to watch *The Irishman* on Netflix. (You know, Martin Scorsese's hit movie that is three and a half hours long and took us a week to finish.) Jana immediately migrates to the middle of the bed right next to me, adding to my feeling of discomfort. I begin to ask myself, "Why does this continue to bother me? Why am I so damn uncomfortable?" I know all the inner reasons why and the fact that I typically avoid intimacy. But this is one of those nights when I hit my breaking point, and later on when we turn over to go to bed, I begin to pray about it: I need help, I need help.

I HATE the fact that I get uncomfortable around intimate moments with my wife. I don't want to be like that anymore. I was asking God to help me. *I don't like this part of me, I don't want to be uncomfortable. God, what can I do?*

This story brings us to the question: What do you do when you need help? What do you do when you feel alone? Who, or what, do you turn to when you feel lost? Everyone's answer will be different, depending on the situation at hand. When we were going through the worst of times, we honestly didn't know where to turn at first. The pain was so great, the sadness so vast, and the agony so incredibly immense, we felt as if no one could understand or relate to us. No literature, no therapist, no person could give us answers, let alone be the support we needed. Admittedly, one of our first problems was that we didn't know where to look for answers. The second problem was that we were looking in all the wrong places. The only person who could ultimately be what we needed was God.

We aren't discrediting any of the literature we've read, the professional help we've received, or the support of our friends and families. We're merely stating that going to them first wasn't the answer for us. When we did, we were on fact-finding missions, trying to fill our heads with inspirational tidbits that would make us feel better—all the while trying to exercise control over the situation. However, we found out that none of that was going to help until we learned to let go. It wasn't our job to find the answers; it was our job to give all the power over to God with the goal of understanding. Until we understood what was going on within ourselves as individuals and as a couple, we couldn't find any of those answers we were yearning for.

I've always believed in God. I was raised Catholic and grew up going to Mass every Sunday. As I entered into my adult life, I didn't attend Mass often but still maintained a connected relationship with God. In my middle twenties, though, I felt more and more distance from God. I wasn't praying very often or doing any kind of spiritual work. Knowing what I know about myself now, I realize that it was because of how lost I had become in my addiction. I would have felt like a hypocrite going to church or praying to God given how I was living my life. I was valuing all the wrong things: acting out sexually with new women constantly, watching pornography, and not being faithful in relationships. I was lost, and I felt lost. To this day, there is a specific memory I think back on that shows how unmanageable and sad my life had become. Let me set the scene for you.

It was a morning in late winter or early spring. As I lay in bed slowly becoming more and more conscious, I felt a tugging at my bedside. It was my (then) five-month-old pup Chance (who now is almost seven years old). I sat up in bed, and for some reason a rush of feelings came over me and I asked myself, out loud mind you, "How come I'm not waking up the happiest person in the world?"

Now let me explain why I thought I should have been feeling like the happiest person in the world back then. Months before that morning, at twenty-six years old, I had just purchased my first home—a 4,420-square-foot corner row house in the beautiful Baltimore neighborhood of Fell's Point. It had just been gutted and renovated before I bought it, so I'm talking a two-tiered rooftop deck, a top-floor master suit, and an elevator. If it wasn't already sweet enough, three of my best friends were living there with me. I also had constant attention from lots of women, money in the bank, great friends, great family, and I was literally living my dream by playing in the NFL.

Now I don't mention all of that in order to boast, but because those are all the things that I allowed to dictate my happiness. I thought that if I had all of that, then there was no reason for me to be unhappy. Yet there I was, waking up feeling empty, unhappy, and lost. Why?

Looking back now, I attribute a lot of it to my lack of connection to God. A bunch of the things I mentioned are still reasonable and healthy contributions to happiness—especially great friends and family. On the surface everything seemed great, but my soul was empty. None of what I thought would control my happiness (money, women, career) filled my soul.

Unfortunately, when Jana and I met, I still placed value on those unhealthy categories that I thought would make me happy. So I continued to fall farther and farther away from my higher power—not even giving that power the time of day anymore. Even when Jana wanted to attend church, I was reluctant because I felt undeserving.

Now let's fast-forward to when everything happened and all of my lies and poor decisions of the previous years were out on the table. Even though I went to rehab and joined a twelve-step program for sex addiction, any twelve-step program revolves around spirituality, and I still felt completely undeserving of God's love. It wasn't until Jana and I started praying out loud together that I began to feel somewhat deserving again. One could look at this as a kind of codependency, but I have experienced the power that praying together with your partner can have on you and your relationship.

There's something so vulnerable about praying. You're opening yourself up to your higher power, and when you do this with someone else, you're opening yourself up to that person as well. When Jana and I started praying together—on our knees and out loud—it was a little uncomfortable at first because of how exposed we felt. But the more we did it, the more comfortable we got. This wasn't quiet praying to ourselves, hoping that we'd be praying about the same things. No, this was speaking our words out into the universe for all to hear—especially God and each other.

Praying Out Loud . . . Together

We may not be experts on faith and God, but boy are we experts on working at our communication. And praying to God is just a kind of communication. Praying may seem awkward and uncomfortable at first—it definitely was for us when we first started. But over time, you'll get more comfortable and it will become a part of you. And plenty of research has supported that old saying "the family that prays together, stays together."

When we heard about some of that research, it encouraged us to start praying more regularly. We had fallen into the same trap that lots of other people do when it comes to their spirituality or higher power. We had relied on prayer a ton early on in the dark days of our relationship, but when the light started to shine on us a bit more, we let up on the gas. Not only have we started praying together again more, but we've also started going to church regularly. Tyler VanderWeele, a professor at the Harvard T. H. Chan School of Public Health, where much of his research focuses on religion and health, noted in 2016 that his own research and that of others have found that people who attend religious services have "greater marital stability" and are about 30 to 50 percent less likely to get divorced than people who don't attend religious services.

Of course, you have to decide what's best for your relationship because it's up to you two, no one else. But here are our three spiritual practices that we think lead to and support a better and long-lasting relationship:

1. Pray together.

2. Go to church together.

3. Let God in.

Jana

I'm not gonna lie; this one has always been really hard for me. I stared at a blank page for quite some time before I wrote any words. It's not that I don't believe in God, because I do. It's just that my faith has had its ups and downs. I was raised Catholic, but some people might have called my family "Chreasters," that is, we were Christians who went to church only on Christmas Eve and (don't forget!) Easter. As a kid, I was also forced to go to catechism every week, not because it was important to my parents but because they thought they would look like bad parents if I didn't go. Truthfully, all I can remember from that time is making my mom rush home so I wouldn't miss *MacGyver*.

So as you can see, church wasn't a big part of my childhood. Then enter my adolescent years and my struggles with my father. I never understood why someone would pray to a "Father" because based on the experience I had, a father wasn't a reliable figure.

Even through my parents' eventual divorce, my leaving home, and my pursuing a career out West, I never truly prayed to God. I might have prayed once when my high school sweetheart broke up with me, swearing to God that I would never miss another day of school if we got back together. And I know I promised God a time or two that I would never have sex again if my period would just please come. But all joking aside, you get my point. I never turned to God during hard times.

Like I said before, I tended to find solace in men—trying to find that "father figure" but all the while never feeling accepted. People would tell me, "Pray about it," and I would feel so uncomfortable with that. Men were always the ones letting me down, or abusing me, so to pray to this "Father" seemed twisted in my mind. It wasn't until I hit my late twenties that I realized I could create the picture of what my God looks like, and from there I essentially started to date God. I started to let God guide me, which is what I have valued the most with my relationship with him. I would be mad at him, question him, love him, and realize that no matter what, he is always there for me.

The thing I have found out with God is that it might not all make sense, but there's always a reason behind everything, and God is always there to help guide you if you let him. The night I found out about Michael's infidelity, I was on my knees sobbing and praying to understand what had just happened. You might be wondering how I found out? Well, a very close friend of mine was very honest with me and said, "I think he's cheating on you." She formed that opinion from the countless hours I spent downloading her on weird behaviors that Mike had been doing the past few months. I still didn't believe it. But one day during a show in Orlando, I decided to look through the phone bill, and there it was. Numbers that didn't add up, and when I called them, the web started to unravel. I was on my hands and knees, devastated. I was lost and utterly betrayed. Our marriage in that instant became the furthest thing from real, and when I returned to Nashville after my show, it was just me and our baby girl. There were so many cry-myself-to-sleep nights mixed with rage-filled days. I had friends stopping over to make sure I was eating, to help me with Jolie. It was as if someone had died. And that's when I truly started to pray again. That praying hasn't stopped since, and I know I couldn't have gotten through the past few years without my relationship with God. But, damn, is he constantly throwing me curveballs, like the night I almost filed divorce papers because Mike had relapsed. A little backstory: We got into a massive fight, he stormed out of our LA house, and the next thing I knew I was showing up at a hotel instead of the "other women" he had called for. In that moment, in that seedy hotel room in Studio City, I had had enough.

I called the lawyers and said, "This is it, I'm finally done, please file the papers." In my heart of hearts, I believed I couldn't handle it anymore, and I felt calm in my decision. My lawyer, who was based in Nashville, called me later that Friday afternoon and said, "We can't file the papers till Monday because the courts are closing and we won't get them in on time." I begged her to pull some strings, but she couldn't. That's when I prayed to God. I kept saying, "Dear God, please, please show me a sign. Give me a reason to stay. Give me something to keep fighting for if it's the path I'm supposed to be on. Show me that this relationship is worth fighting for. Show me that sign please." The next morning, I found out I was pregnant with our second child, Jace.

I've never shared this story before. I think in that moment I became a believer. Some people may call it just a fluke, a coincidence, but I know what it was, and that's all that matters. I asked God for help, I asked God for clarity, and though God in no way, shape, or form told me what to do, God gave me a sign of hope. That glimpse of hope was everything that I needed, and more. Those two dark lines on that pregnancy test were God's way of saying,

Just take a minute to really think through this, and that's what I did. My lawyer called me on Monday and asked whether I was set to file, and I told her I needed to put it on hold. In that moment, I wasn't sure what was going to happen—I still considered leaving and raising my kids as a single mom, but what I knew, regardless, was that I was going to have that baby.

It took a few good months working through Mike's relapse for me to feel calm in my decision to stay and work together. As each month passed and my belly got bigger and our relationship continued to get healthier, my heart felt calmer and clearer that I was making the right decision. I saw for the first time the change in Michael. He was different. He was stronger and more present in his recovery; he had more empathy and more patience, which allowed me to put my sword down. When the moments of weakness or worry crept in, I kept going back to God and remembering what I had prayed for. I had asked for a sign, and God gave us our sweet baby boy Jace, whose name comes from the Greek meaning "healer." Which is exactly what he has been for us. Jace helped us heal, and Michael and I gave him a family.

Spiritual Forgiveness/Self-Forgiveness

I knew we were going to have to write about this topic, but honestly, I've been terrified to do it. There are a lot of days when I just don't feel like I deserve forgiveness. A lot of that has to do with "not feeling good enough" and the heavy shame

I carry around my actions. If I had a friend or a loved one in my situation, I would try to persuade him that he deserves to forgive himself. Especially after seeing his work and dedication to the program over several years. As much as I have tried to affirm myself, as much as twelve-step meetings have helped me feel better, as much as my sponsor and brothers in the program have lifted me up over the years, I still have felt undeserving of forgiveness. Finally I decided I needed to do something different in order to start chipping away at that shame and feel some self-forgiveness. That was when I decided to let God back in my life.

It was in rehab when I began to open up to the idea of a higher power again. Having a higher power is a pillar in any twelve-step program, and as I was raised Catholic, God was and is mine. Now, it's a bit easier to lean into religion when everything in my life has gone to shit. Even more so when I was on the verge of losing everything and completely shut off from the outside world, all while spending those sixty days in southern Mississippi during the heart of the summer. Yeah, probably a good time to find God again. Joking aside, I did begin to find him again, dropping to my knees and praying out loud every morning and night while there. It's something I still do every morning.

Before I move forward with this topic, it's imperative for me to touch on rehab for a moment. I have been reluctant in doing so, but Jana has been encouraging me to open up about it. As I just stated, I spent sixty days down in Hattiesburg, Mississippi (seventy total away from Jolie). I lived on a mini campus that had a twelve-foot high fence all the way around it, with about two dozen other men anywhere from age eighteen to sixty-plus. It was a traumatizing experience, for both Jana and me, but I have difficulty putting into words the level of pain, sadness, and several other emotions I felt during that time. Having said all that, I know it was what I needed. I couldn't be where I am today if it wasn't for that time. And most importantly, I wouldn't have God in my life like I do now if it wasn't for that experience.

Shortly after being released from rehab I decided I needed to work on forgiving myself in order to rid myself of the seemingly immovable blanket of shame I was wearing. So, because I was raised Catholic, I sought out a local church and their confessional hours. I sat there with the priest, face-to-face, a bit hesitant that even while in God's house I may be judged for my actions. As I began to share, I was quickly overrun with emotions and at the same time incredibly cleansed. I walked out of that church completely exhausted—emotionally drained and physically fatigued—but spiritually fulfilled. After that confession was the first time in my young recovery that I said to myself, "Maybe I do deserve forgiveness."

I wish I could sit here and tell you that from that moment my recovery program has been flawless, but it hasn't. I've had my slips of dishonesty and lack of integrity. I even had a situation that Jana and I call a relapse back in February 2018. Jana just filled you in on that situation above. Ultimately I got to the place where I hit the "fuck it" button and, due to not working a consistently healthy recovery program, I was willing to blow my life up all over again. I truly believe that God stepped in. He knew Jana was pregnant, he knew we were meant to have Jace, he knew that we deserve to be together, and he knew that us sharing our story could help other couples continue to believe and to fight.

All of this has now come full circle. In February 2020 I got baptized again. This time at Crosspoint Church, a nondenominational church with Christian teachings here in the Greater Nashville area that Jana and I attend weekly. After four years of fighting my shame, my demons, my secrets, and my lies, I was fully ready to recommit my life to Christ—to admit that I need him in my life, that I love him, and that finally for the first time in over ten years, I *know* that he loves me without any exception, and that I too deserve his love.

Sex Addiction

For those of you who don't know Jana and me very well, it's important for me to touch briefly on the topic of sex addiction. I am a sex addict, and it is a real thing. It took a while for me to truly comprehend the meaning of that, let alone accept it. Some of you may furrow your brows in confusion or judgment, and that's okay. Sexual addiction is still about ten to fifteen years away from being understood—just as alcoholism and Alcoholics Anonymous were confusing concepts for most people when AA was first founded back in the 1930s.

Sex was my drug. I used it to feel "good enough," to wash away feelings that I didn't want to sit with or didn't know how to express, and to escape the pain of depression—most of the same types of reasons people have for abusing drugs or alcohol. I absolutely HATE that this is a part of who I am, but it is, and I'm stuck with it. There is no "cure" for addiction, only a solution. I'm sure a lot of you reading this have been directly affected by addiction in some way, so y'all probably get it. You've most likely witnessed the pain and shame that surrounds the addict and those closest to him or her. And I'm truly sorry that you have to feel any of that pain.

I still live with the immense shame and guilt of my actions, and I will for a long time. But slowly, the deeper I get into recovery, the more that shame dissipates. And that dissipation will continue only as long as I continue to go to twelve-step meetings and work through those twelve steps.

I want to be very clear about something: society has had the nerve to call sex addiction a "married man's excuse." To which I say, bull . . . (wait for it) . . . shit. Addiction is not an excuse at all, and I make sure to never use it as such. However, it *is* an explanation. It explains why I've behaved the way I have in the past. These twelve-step meetings for sex addicts include men and women of all ages, races, marital status, sexual orientation, and profession. So to hear it being labeled as an excuse is infuriating for those of us who are trying to change our lives and get out of that powerless, unmanageable, dark, sad, and painful chaos we have lived in.

Forgiving

Jana

I remember being a teen and asking my mom, "How did you forgive Dad?" I've always remembered her response, but it didn't make sense to me for quite some time. She said, "Forgiving isn't for the other person, it's for you." This made zero sense to my sixteen-year-old self because moving on seemed unbearable. Problem is, though, when you're in the middle of a volcano erupting, forgiveness looks impossible and uncomfortably vulnerable.

Thinking back on what my mom said to me, I knew that the only way I could possibly let go of the pain and hurt that Mike caused in my life was to forgive him. I knew that by forgiving him, I could start to heal. Forgiving doesn't mean forgetting; it just means that you're ready to start picking up the pieces. In the end, forgiveness is something you can ask God to help you do because he is the king of forgiveness. So ask him to help you. As it says in the Bible, "Be kind and compassionate to one another, forgiving each other, just as in Christ God forgave you" (Ephesians 4:32).

If you're needing to forgive yourself, I have also been there, so I see you and I can relate. Forgiving yourself is just as important as forgiving others. Granted, it can be one of the hardest things you do. There are some things in my past that I truly am too ashamed to share with certain people. I buried them so deeply in my soul that for years I told no one. The somewhat silver lining in doing as much therapy as I've done is that I had to face what I shoved down in my soul and forgive myself in order to move on, in order to grow.

I think Maya Angelou said it best: "You forgive yourself for every failure because you are trying to do the right thing. God knows that and you know it. Nobody else may know it." Ultimately, my hope for you when you're forgiving yourself is that it makes you stronger because you don't deserve to hold on to the suffering that not forgiving yourself causes you and your body. Let God help you because no matter what, God is there for you. God doesn't judge you, and God forgives you.

What If You're Spiritual but Your Partner Isn't?

This can be a tough question, especially if you are strong in certain beliefs and your partner goes on about, for instance, the big bang and conspiracy theories. We encourage you to have early conversations about religious beliefs if they're important to you. If your partner isn't spiritual and that doesn't bother you, then be like Mahatma Gandhi, who said, "We must be the change we wish to see in the world."

And who knows? Maybe if your partner sees how your spirituality helps you be happy and fulfilled, he or she will be more inclined to hear you out and see what your beliefs and practices are all about.

Our Love Road Map

Here's the deal. We wouldn't be able to be where we are today if it weren't for accepting our lives on God's terms. Early in our reconciliation we were stuck on *how the fuck*, *who the fuck*, and *what the fucking fucking fuck*. All of which were out of our control at that point. We couldn't fix the past, and for those of you who don't know, time travel doesn't exist yet. Trust us, we did the research. But seriously, it took us a long time to reach a healthy level of acceptance. We can speak with the utmost experience, though, that when we did, our lives began to change for the better.

Acceptance is what jump-started what we call our "love road map." Here's how that looks for us:

Acceptance = Trust

Trust = Love

Love = Vulnerability

Vulnerability = Intimacy

Intimacy = Kindness

This road map started our path of reconciliation. So for us, the order of our map and the pairings of words are specific to our relationship and everything we were going through. Let us explain.

Once we hit that healthy level of acceptance, we were able to say, "Okay, this is our life now, and we trust God's plan, so let's figure this out." It was more about trusting God's plan than it was about trusting one another. But through accepting and trusting God, we were able to accept and trust one another again.

With trust being reestablished, love was able to be more apparent in our daily interactions with one another. It's near impossible to love someone you don't trust, so for our recovery, that was imperative in order for love to flourish.

After more love continued to fill our relationship, then our vulnerability had more room to grow. Not many people can be openly vulnerable with someone they don't love and trust, which is why we needed those first steps before we could be completely open with our feelings.

Vulnerability had its challenges because there was so much pain, hurt, shame, and guilt surrounding our relationship and our hearts. It took a lot of time and practice before we were able to get back to having intimate moments with each other. We aren't talking just sex here; intimacy is so much more than sex. It could be anything from holding hands to intentional time and conversations. For us, it looked a lot of different ways. But admittedly, sex was one of the most important for sure.

Eventually that intimacy grew into kindness. Now, that might sound a bit elementary or simplistic because "kindness" seems like such a common concept. But unfortunately, there wasn't a regular dose of kindness between us during the early years of reconciliation. We thought that if we could get to that place of being soft and kind with one another again, then maybe we would have made it through the worst of it. It was almost our light at the end of the tunnel. We still have our dark days and our struggles—everyone does. But the fact that we're back to the place where we can be kind and soft with one another is a gigantic win for us.

Your love road map may look completely different from ours, but we recommend including those words in your road map. It's about what works for you and what steps you need to take in order to reach the next level. We hope your route is smoother than ours has been. Happy traveling!

Hand It Over to God

God works in mysterious ways, doesn't he. It helps that we're both believers in a higher power, but it hasn't been easy. We have tested, challenged, and questioned our spiritual relationship—bouncing around in that metaphysical pinball machine, bouncing back and forth, back and forth throughout our lives until we found our lane, all the while not knowing exactly what to believe, and at times questioning whether God was actually there. We understand now that it wasn't about our waiting on God to show up. He was always there, allowing us to make our mistakes, have our questions, and commit our sins. God never left our side but simply waited for the moment we realized that we don't have to hold on to all of our pain, sadness, sins, regrets, questions, anxiety, or depression. We realize that we don't have to live trying to control all that negativity. We don't have power over all those issues, but we do have the power to hand everything over to God.

That is what we try to do more and more these days in our life together. We strive to stop controlling and to start living more, allowing God to take the negative from us and for us. We heard a powerful message from our pastor this past Sunday: when we say, "God, I'm over it," he responds with, "I'm all over it." Powerful, right? Reread that and let it sink in.

Spirituality is customizable, and there shouldn't be too many rules. So no matter who you choose to follow—God, Allah, Zeus, Santa Claus, or a nine-pound-six-ounce baby Jesus—it's all about what makes you feel the most connected, what fills your heart and soul, and what gives you a spiritual purpose to live for more than just yourself. We have a more connected relationship with our higher power now because we finally feel like we made the choice. We weren't told what to believe or who to believe in. Our lives led us here, and we finally decided to let go and let God.

9 It Takes Two

Jana

It was October 2, 2016. I remember that day like it was yesterday. I was at camera blocking for *Dancing with the Stars* when I got a text from my publicist Nicole to call her immediately. My heart dropped to the floor because that time of my life was pure chaos and madness so I rarely was getting good news. Why was it chaos and madness, you ask? Well, I had signed on to do the show a few weeks after Michael had left for sexual addiction rehab. To audiences in America, we had separated and he had gone away, but that was the extent of what I had shared. You might be thinking, Why would you sign up for *Dancing with the Stars* when your world was falling apart? Yeah, I often questioned that too, but I needed a healthy escape, and *Dancing* was it. However, the outside

world and noise seemed to dampen it, and that day when I called
Nicole back was no exception.

"Hey Nicole, what's up?"

"I don't have good news."

"Okay, what happened?"

"I have been on the phone with the Us Weekly *editor all day; I
have been trying to get them to not run the story but, I'm sorry,
Jana, there is nothing I can do. I've tried everything."*

"What does that mean?"

*"Someone told the magazine everything, and they're running the
cover story tomorrow: 'Married to a Sex Addict.'"*

Us Against the World

The thing about any coupledom is that there are always outside
influences. Whether positive, negative, beneficial, or detrimental,
they exist. It's human nature to be swayed by the environment
around us; we are adaptive creatures. What kind of outside influences
affect your relationship? And do they do more harm than good?

Living a public life, we're no strangers to the pressure of outside
influences—especially since we had to deal with the controversy of
Mike's addiction and rehab story publicly. That situation brought
on a flood of haters, critics, and judgment for both of us. Some
people offered sympathy and empathy, too, but early on, those
people were few and far between.

All of that negative energy added to the emotional distance between us, but we ended up coming to the conclusion that if we had any chance to move forward together, we had to become united. At that point, it truly felt like it was us against the world. Now, we aren't sitting here claiming that from that moment on our bond was unwavering; we still had to battle outside pressures. And that shit was hard. But having that mindset was imperative to getting to the place where we are today. We understand that at the end of the day, only two people matter—US. After that, it's Jolie and Jace. (And maybe after them it would be our dogs, Chance and Waffles.) We are Team Caussin, and if you aren't on board with us going in the same direction, then you can leave.

In our experience and opinion, that's how all relationships should be.

Again, it's natural for your feelings or opinions to be swayed at times. But as long as you and your partner communicate and are on the same page about your feelings and life path, then that's all that matters. Don't let someone else drive a wedge between y'all. That goes for family members as well. We get that family may complicate things, and you may need to dance a bit more delicately around those relationships. But here's the deal: they are your family, they love you, and at the end of the day they are going to support you and follow your lead. If they don't, then don't be afraid to have those tough conversations. So, whether it's a family member, a friend, or someone else trying to negatively influence you, then fuck 'em. You don't need them.

Teammates

We've often heard our therapists encourage us to treat each other more like teammates. That concept didn't land with us immediately. It took us some time to process and understand what they meant. Maybe it was because we were so worried about being "equal" with everything we did, and that's not what teammates do. And then it hit us. Every team is made up of players who all have a specific job to do, and they do it. Sure, one person may contribute more than others, but ultimately, nothing can be accomplished by one individual. Everyone has a role to play.

The same goes for a healthy relationship. One person can't singularly run the show (as much as one might try at times). We need that teammate or partner in order to stay balanced in our effort. Some days we might not be the team's best player, or maybe we're riding the bench a bit more during a period of our lives. But at the end of the day we're still a team, which means we still need to show up and put in the work. On any team, just because one player may be contributing more at one time doesn't mean the others don't practice as hard. They all still show up and play their role.

Let's face it, Rob Base and DJ E-Z Rock said it the best: "It takes two to make a thing go right." (We'll let you finish the song in your head because we know you get the point.) But, it just does! We get asked all the time, "How do you know whether or not to stay?" The number one response you'll get from us is, *It takes two.* It takes two people in a relationship to fight, love, go through the mud, and make it work.

We've all been in relationships where maybe the other person isn't putting in the work, or maybe that person was you. Ultimately, that relationship can't continue to grow because there isn't effort on both sides. It becomes so one-sided that it's impossible to hold up the tilting foundation. But it's not easy to let that fall down. Loving someone and just letting that fall through your hands is a heartbreaking time, especially when you don't understand why. At the end of the day, there's only so much that you can hold on to, and in order for the relationship to flourish, you both have to be willing to do the work and do it as a team.

We aren't saying that if your partner is having a bad day and isn't working as a teammate then your relationship is doomed. There's no way to be perfect in every issue that may arise, but it's important to be mindful of the work you're doing. That's not to keep score because keeping score isn't good either. It's more about keeping your side of street clean (see Chapter 2) and doing your work as an individual and as a partner.

It's particularly important to work as a team during arguments. That helps lead you to The Good Fight. You know your stuff, you know your issues, and dammit, we know you know your partner's hot spots that get her or him more upset. Being mindful that you're being constructive in your arguments rather than tearing down the home team is a win in our book.

It's also important to work as a team in parenting. Remember how annoying it was when both of your parents would agree that you couldn't go to your friend's house or have that last piece of double fudge chocolate brownie? Now that we're parents, we see how working as a team benefits the kids and us. Yeah, maybe we'll say, "Oh come on, let them have one more brownie," but at the end of the day, it's best to work together and stay on the same page and team.

Jana

I know who told *Us Weekly* about Mike. I know because when I was reading the article, there was a piece of information that I had told only ONE person. To make matters worse, he had been in our wedding. At the time, it felt like another kick in the gut from someone I loved and someone I thought I knew.

The three months I spent alone while Mike was at rehab were consumed with a lot of friends giving me their advice. Many of them questioned why in the world I hadn't filed for divorce yet, but what they repeated the most to me was that no matter what I decided, they would have my back and support me. That's how I knew my friends were my true friends, and to this day when shit pops up, they always say, "No matter what, we've got your back and support you." And some, like my friend Kristen, will say, "Just let me know when you need help hiding the body."

Have I had hard conversations with my friends? Absolutely. They are by no means enabling a bad situation. I know they will tell me when I'm overreacting and I know they will step in if it gets to that point, but the fact of the matter is your relationship is your relationship. Your TRUE friends are going to be there for you, have your back, and support you. That goes for family, too. My family told me, "If you love him, we love him."

It took both of us to work as a team, though, and sometimes that isn't easy. But at the end of the day we were, and we are, fighting for each other—fighting The Good Fight. Fighting for our marriage. Fighting for our family. Ultimately, we know our goal, and that's to keep showing up for each other and this relationship. There may be times when Mike is doing a better job at communicating, but just like any team member, he's going to try to get me up when I'm hurt and to show me what we're fighting for. And I'll do the same for him. There would have been no way in hell this would have worked if we hadn't picked each other up along the way and worked together.

I wrote the following quotation in my journal to help me during the times I need the extra reminder that it truly takes two: "A relationship can only work between two people who are totally present and dedicated to one another, despite any outward distractions or internal problems. You're either in it together or not in it at all."

Keeping Score

Well, keeping score is a fun topic. We've all done it, and maybe still do, at times. Even if we don't consciously keep score, we may still find a way to do it subconsciously. It seems to be human nature, a way that our minds learn from past experiences, categorize those experiences, and then make judgments based on them. But is that fair, especially in a relationship? Hell no, of course it's not fair. Judging our partner based on the moments that person may not meet our expectations is a recipe for disaster. If we all focused on #Winning in our relationships, then we would merely destroy them one after the other.

Here are some negative effects that keeping score can have on a relationship that we have noticed and experienced:

JEEP FOCUS (MISGUIDED FOCUS): What actions of your partner do you focus on the most in your relationship? Do you focus on what he is doing or what she is not doing? Think about it like this. Say you've always wanted to buy a Jeep Wrangler and you just recently started looking for one. What are you going to notice more when you're driving around town? Exactly, Jeep Wranglers. So in your relationship, if you are caught up in keeping score, what are you going to be primarily focused on? We know you know the answer here. Your partner could do ten things right, but if you're focused on what he does wrong, then that one "wrong" act can trump what he's been doing right. Not a fun way to live for either of you, is it?

WHO CRANKED UP THE PASSIVENESS?: When we've gotten caught in that score-keeping loop in the past, we really noticed our passiveness spike. It's like we were vultures waiting for that roadkill in order to swoop in and start pecking at it—feeling like we were justified and finally had the other pegged with what he or she may have done "wrong."

IT'S A BIRD, IT'S A PLANE, IT'S SUPERMA . . . NOPE, IT'S JUST EMPATHY FLYING OUT THE WINDOW: In our experience, holding on to these moments in order to keep score resulted in only resentment (see Chapter 2). And when you're filled with resentment, it's almost impossible to show your partner any empathy. It's difficult to acknowledge that your partner may be having a bad day when you're gradually preparing that preemptive strike, ready to push that "launch" button.

We get that keeping score can be a natural habit; just like everything else in a relationship, it's going to take practice and conscious effort to change. We don't get this right all the time at all, but we try to redirect our attention to what we're doing for one another rather than what we aren't. It's important to remember that we aren't saying you have to let everything go that bothers or frustrates you, but there are different/healthier ways to handle those feelings.

Mike

Being someone who takes a lot of things in life personally and has a tendency to get defensive, I have focused a lot of my attention on staying in the present more—trying not to allow "keeping score" of past issues to affect me. When Jana says something that causes me to feel parented, controlled, or unequal, then I write down the scenario and how I feel about it in the notes section on my phone.

I have a few reasons for doing this. First of all, history shows that my past responses in those situations do not typically come out the way I would like—that is, I'm usually defensive. Second, I tend to make generalized statements in response, like "you always" or "you never." Third, if I don't say anything in that moment or if I don't write something down, then I would most likely pick a fight at the next opportunity I had. So, it helps me to write down the scenario and my feelings about it. This way, instead of pushing those feelings down or forgetting what happened, I can try to bring them up later, and I have my notes to remind me what happened and how I felt. I usually process these feelings with my therapist, our couples therapist, or even my twelve-step sponsor before I bring things back up with Jana. This helps me get grounded and experience some empathy and not be stuck solely on my interpretation of a situation.

The key is to make sure you are actually setting the feelings aside for later, rather than merely pushing them down. That's where resentment grows.

He/She Is Not Your Enemy

Keeping score can make it feel like the other person is your enemy, right? It's not like you're going to be keeping a mental note of what she's doing that pisses you off while thinking at the same time, "Wow, I'm so lucky, and I love her so much." The thing is, we get why this shit is hard. We're living with another human being who in many ways is completely different from us. And sometimes that difference looks like the enemy. That's why for us it has to be a constant and conscious practice to redirect our minds toward lifting each other up and appreciating one another as opposed to criticizing and putting each other down. Because has "winning" an argument in your relationship ever made anything better?

We're striving to create and maintain in our household a consistently safe and inviting environment for each other and for our kids. We always want the other to come to us if a feeling or topic or comment needs to be expressed. We've found that the best areas for practicing this are the "unavoidables"—the discussions around kids, expenses, lifestyle, and moral principles. These are all things that need to be discussed in a relationship. So why not use them to practice lifting each other up and compromising?—as opposed to putting your foot down to make a point. These kinds of discussions and compromises showed us that it's possible to carry over kindness and understanding into other parts of our relationship.

We didn't always handle them with as much grace as we do now. We often would purposely hit those "hot buttons" just to rile the other person up. At times, doing that seemed harmless, but as time wore on, we noticed more and more resentful feelings coming up any time the other felt like "poking the bear." Maybe it's just the natural competitiveness in us that wants to get in the other's head at times, but that shit can eventually wear down a relationship.

No matter how well we or y'all do this, we are all still teammates with our partner, and at the end of the day teammates are still capable of fighting all the damn time. But when it's game time, all those feelings of difference get set aside in order to achieve the common goal. So in a relationship, we see life being the game, and our common goal is to make it through safely, happily, and most importantly, together. We chose one another, we committed to each other, so we are going to claw and scratch and fight (even with each other at times) The Good Fight to achieve our common goal.

It Takes Two to Apologize

We touched on some of the most effective ways to apologize back in Chapter 2. But we think it's important to remind y'all (but mostly ourselves) that it takes two to apologize, just like it takes two to fight. Now, we aren't saying you should apologize if you didn't do anything wrong, but in most cases, you probably played a part in the story, which means owning up to your side of the street, like we also discussed in Chapter 2. It's frustrating if only one of you does the apologizing, and granted, maybe one of you is causing more of the arguments. But we're challenging you to take a look in the mirror and return that apology to your partner. When two people can come together and own up to their parts and say how they could have done things better, they can build a stronger foundation for the relationship.

We also want to mention that when your partner is apologizing, it's important for you to be receptive to that apology. Holding a grudge is never healthy. Having said that, don't accept an apology just to accept it and move on. It's a major blow when your partner "says" she accepts your apology but then throws it in your face later. Both of you need to be purposeful with the interactions around an apology. Don't just go through the motions. This is such a great opportunity to leave a situation in a good place and become more connected.

Do Women Apologize More Than Men?

We googled whether women apologize more than men and found a 2019 article by Amy Morin from Inc.com called "Women Really Do Apologize More Than Men. Here's Why (and It Has Nothing to Do with Men Refusing to Admit Wrongdoing)." The title says it all: the fact that women apologize more has nothing to do with the perception that men are stubborn or bull-headed. But it has everything to do with the fact that men and women have very different views on what deserves an apology. Women say "I'm sorry" more often because they consider more things as needing or requiring an apology. Morin points out that women may want to think about this, because apologies "may reinforce the notion that you've done something wrong." At the same time, if people don't acknowledge their mistakes, they may hurt their relationships. She writes, "Apologizing more often might be the key to maintaining healthier relationships over the long-term."

Lastly

Sadly, people who can't find their groove working well as a team in a relationship find themselves getting to an unavoidable end. But if you can't work together, then you're both most likely better off apart, and that's okay. Some people just aren't meant to coexist alongside one another.

So to summarize our outlook, here's what we want to leave y'all with:

- If there's a "winner," then you're both ultimately losers.

- Is your personal motivation to be right or to be heard?

- Empathy generates understanding.

- If you know your partner's buttons, avoid them. Don't push them.

We're continuing to strive to be better teammates. Admittedly, it's really difficult at times. But at the end of the day, we chose each other and we've made this decision to make it work. And to do that, we believe it's necessary to live and work as a unified team. As Abe Lincoln famously said, "A house divided against itself, cannot stand."

10 Make the Time

Jana

I've always been a big believer in and big advocate of date nights and intentional time together. I know, surprise surprise. Maybe it's the fact that it feeds my needs to feel wanted and chosen, but I also know the importance of having that intentional time and what it does for a relationship. Over the past few years with Mike I have sometimes pointed out to him that even though he made time for his friends, and he made sure his medical sales job was a priority, I felt like he didn't intentionally make time to spend with me. To him, I sound like a needy nag. To me, I'm craving that time to connect and nourish our relationship. Mike felt that I was saying he wasn't good enough and that our nights at home weren't enough.

Let me rewind and let you into our nighttime routine . . .

5:30 p.m.—Dinner time. This is when we beg Jolie to eat her spiral zucchini noodles and tell her that if she just eats that one bite of spinach, she can get a piece of chocolate. Then there's Jace—throwing his bowls filled with perfectly cut veggies and fruit and then swatting the rest off the high chair plate.

6:30—Bath time. It's usually a hit or a miss with the kids. They either play and have lots of fun, or it's bloodcurdling screams coming from both of them because they got water in their eyes (even though the night before they were totally fine with getting water dumped on them . . . insert major mom eye roll).

7:00—Pj time followed by book time, which consists of reading any unicorn book for Jolie twice and Jace's favorite and total tearjerker *You're Here for a Reason*. After books, our nighttime prayers and goodnight songs and a big hug and kiss to cap the day off.

Usually by 7:30 the kids are asleep. Jolie will have come out at least five times for water, to say hi, to ask for a hug, or to tell us she's scared or has to go potty.

By 8:00 p.m. I've cleaned up the kitchen, scrubbed the noodles off the wall (probably from the previous night), and successfully thrown myself into a pair of my finest sweatpants and sweatshirt. By 8:05 I have the TV on and a very large pour of red wine in hand.

On this specific night, Mike walks in and plops down on the couch next to me. A certain negative energy is in the air when he comes in, which in all actuality is my fault. Mike looks over to me and asks, "You good?" I think to myself, *Honestly, I don't know whether I'm good. I'm tired and if I'm honest with myself, I don't feel pretty, I'm in sweats, I'm exhausted, I feel like I'm just a washed-up version of myself beat up from the day with the kids.*

But instead, I say, "Yup, I'm fine." Which in Jana fashion is incredibly passive. Then I ask, "When's the last time we had a date night?" To which he asks, "Why is it not enough to have me here on the couch with you?" He points out that we are spending time together right there and then. To me, though, watching another rose ceremony of *The Bachelorette* isn't spending intentional time together. It's just another routine Monday where he happened to plop on the couch to see what bozo she would hand the rose to.

No doubt, I loved that he sat next to me that night, and I truly love nothing more than those lazy do-nothing sorts of nights when we don't say a word and just unwind, and I LOVE our family nights so much and I wouldn't trade those nights for anything. It's not that it's not enough. It's not that he's not enough. It's just that I believe that intentional time sets you up for relationship success. I always tell Mike that we can sit on the couch together, but let's have a conversation other than "How did the baby go down?" Let's make an intentional effort to talk.

Intentional Time

What do you do in your life that is intentional? Every one of us has at least one thing that we either preplan, do deliberately, calculate before we do it, or consciously do on purpose. All of these fall under the umbrella of *intention*. We are so busy, and life is short, so how do you currently spend your time, and how do you *intend* to use the time you have left?

We all have our different interests and values, which help us sculpt our personalities and choose the people we want to be around. But one thing that stays fairly constant across the board, regardless of personalized interests, is relationships. Most people strive to share their life with another person. So if we are deliberately seeking someone to be our life partner, then why, when we finally find one, don't we set aside intentional time with that person?

We make time for work, we make time for friends, and we make time for our kids, but what about for each other? If you are married or in a relationship, you'll know that it's easy to get stuck in your daily routine and it's hard to get out of that routine. You might be reading this and thinking, *Well, I'm good, we just had a date night,* and if that's the case, then hell yeah, you get the gold star! But this might not be the case for the next couple—the one who can't remember the last time that they made plans to be together.

We don't mean time at home with the kids and the normal everyday life that you're both living. We're talking about that purposeful time that you both have set aside for each other—that don't-you-dare-check-that-Instagram-account-in-the-middle-of-it kind of night. Just like marriage and relationships, intentional time takes work and practice because naturally, all you and your partner get after another long day of work, kids, and whatever else is that "leftover" time. That leftover time is a great opportunity to spend together. But spending time together and having intentional time with one another are two completely different things—and can be received as such. Which leads us to ask, Shouldn't you proactively take care of the foundation that is holding your relationship up?

You may be thinking to yourself that time spent together is time spent together regardless of how you get there. In some people's brains, this makes total sense. In others', though, spending time together and spending intentional time together are two completely different concepts. We came into our relationship with two different points of view on this, and it's been a struggle at times.

Jana

For the record, intentional time can have many faces. It doesn't have to be some over-the-top date night. Shoot, you don't even have to leave the house if you don't want to. It all centers around *purposeful action*. It can look as simple as staging a different conversation than you would typically have at the end of the day. You do that by asking questions like, "What's going on in your world today?" or "How have you been feeling lately, and is there anything sitting with you that you are upset with or have feelings about?" The object here is to connect and to be each other's friend.

Intentional Conversation Starters

One way to start an intentional conversation is to play a riveting game of "Would You Rather." Here are a few of our favorites just to give you a little push in the right direction so you can spark up a conversation with your partner right now. You're welcome. ;)

- Would you rather eat no candy on Halloween or no turkey on Thanksgiving?
- Would you rather know how you're going to die or when you're going to die?
- Would you rather be the funniest person in the room or the most intelligent?
- Would you rather win $50,000 or let your best friend win $500,000?
- Would you rather have no one show up to your wedding or to your funeral?
- Would you rather speak all languages or be able to speak to all animals?

This may seem silly to some of you, but it's all about making opportunities to open up different levels of conversation with the person you're spending your life with. You may even learn a new thing or two about that person in the process. Which is exactly why the beginning stages of a relationship tend to be the most fun—because you're constantly learning new things about one another. So why not try to re-create that early fun by doing something different, something other than having the same mundane conversations day in and day out.

Whether you're going out on a date night or telling your significant other, "Hey babe, grab a drink and meet me on the couch," it all comes down to your intention. When you're deliberate in your actions, your partner is going to have that blissful feeling of being chosen. Intentional time is dedicated time that you are choosing to spend with one another—not because you have to, not because you live together and have no choice, but because you choose time together over time doing anything else in that moment.

Mike and I have had some issues around intentional time because of our differing personalities, so here's his point of view.

Mike

This has been one of those areas in our relationship that's been a bit more elusive for me to get down. I'm definitely someone who receives feeling chosen or not on an unconscious level. It's never really a top plate issue for me. The way I look at it, Jana chose me when we got married, and I guess that's all I need. My problem lies in questioning whether I'm enough or I'm doing enough, and that's also where our personalities clash. Jana wants more intentional time so she feels chosen and connected, but if she brings it up, then I feel like the times we do spend together or our last date night wasn't enough for her. It's a vicious cycle, with two very contradictory feelings in the same situation. Which is why it's been such a slippery issue to grasp in our marriage.

Let me bring you into my mind a little more, and maybe more men can relate to this mindset—though I'm sure plenty of women can, too. The time that I have left in my day after fulfilling my responsibilities and obligations to my kids, to my job, and to my wife is mine to do with as I choose. I'm saying this as an individual human being, not from atop any high horse. Some days, work needs a little bit more of my time; some nights, when the kids are down, I need to spend some time cleaning up after them or prepping for the next day. Other nights, I choose to spend with Jana. And for me, that could be just sitting on the couch on another Monday night watching the soul-sucking yet entertaining shit show that is *The Bachelorette*. Even though we didn't plan to spend that time together, I'm still making the choice to be with her. I could easily go into the other room and watch something by myself. I could even go sit outside alone with a Manhattan on the rocks and a cigar. Or if I'm feeling productive, I could go work in the garage. (Oh, and when I say "work," I mean work on the 7,541-piece LEGO Special Edition Millennium Falcon that Jana got me for Christmas. Where my fellow nerds at?!) Whatever it is, there are plenty of things I could do on my own without Jana. So from my perspective, choosing to sit with her while watching twenty-four clones of each other fight it out for a flower on a Monday night is intentional time.

I'm bringing this up to illustrate why I have feelings of "not enough" when Jana says that we haven't had intentional time in a while. It's just a hard pill to swallow when I feel like I choose to spend time with her watching TV after the kids are in bed but she doesn't receive it as feeling chosen, she doesn't see it as being truly intentional time.

Now let's get out of my deeper thoughts and back into the world of relationships and marriage. We all know we need to compromise at times for any relationship to work. This is one of those areas where at first I truly thought of it as just a compromise. As time has continued, though, I've learned to understand and experience that having intent and purpose behind time together can enhance those moments. I've learned that there are advantages and disadvantages that coincide when tackling this great conundrum of spending time together and intentional time.

We don't want this to sound overwhelming. You're probably thinking that the last thing you want to do after a long day of work, kids, or dogs is feel like you have to "try" when it comes to your partner. We don't want you to think that what you've been doing isn't enough, or that you have to add one more thing to your plate. It's just about recognizing that your relationship takes work, and strengthening that relationship means you have to put extra time and energy into making sure it's standing steady on solid ground. Also, talk about what intentional time looks like for both of you, and discuss your goals around frequency so you can get on the same page moving forward.

In all honesty, and this may seem biased since this is our book and we're writing an entire chapter on the importance of intentional time, what possible disadvantages could there be to planning intentional time with one another? We have only benefited from it. It's an opportunity to break the cycle of the day-to-day stuff and just enjoy each other's company. Use it as a chance to surprise one another and learn more about the person you love. Intentional time can give you more moments of growth and connectedness, not to mention great possibilities for making memories together. And those of you with children have even more reason to make this a priority because making time for yourselves benefits your children as well. They can see two connected, loving parents who enjoy each other. You are their first exposure to a romantic relationship, so what kind of experience do you want that to be for them?

The only disadvantages that we can foresee are those that come from not having any intentional time. Now, we aren't saying that you're doomed if you don't practice our definition of intentional time. Which, to lay it out simply, is this: *Intentional time is purposeful time set aside for you and your partner to spend together with the goal of growing your love and understanding one another.* And we don't want you to think that after every date night or intended time together, you're supposed to feel closer and more connected. That happens naturally over time. It's about enjoying each other, it's about being friends.

We're sure you've been in a relationship at some point where you've said to yourself, "Is this it?" Asking that question sucks in any relationship, but it's terrifying to think about getting to that point with the person you're choosing to spend your life with. So if you're not implementing opportunities to learn more about each other and grow together, you may get to that point eventually.

It's important to remember why you are being intentional with one another. You must do it for the right reasons, and one person can't be doing it just to make the other happy. That would defeat the whole purpose of inspiring connection. It has to be because it's something you both discuss and decide on for your relationship.

Living with more intention in all aspects of life is something that both of us are trying to get better at. We constantly share things with each other that we want to do or learn in our lives, but often, we catch ourselves saying the same thing most of us do: *I don't have the time*. If writing this chapter has reminded us of anything, it's that the whole idea behind intention isn't whether or not you *have* the time, it's about *making* the time.

Your Own Time

After all this talk about time together, we don't want the concept of time alone to be overlooked. Time for you can be just as vital to you and your relationship as time together. The way we look at your own time is kind of like the idea that you can't truly love someone until you love yourself. We often find ourselves coming back to each other more connected and intimate once we've done work on our own.

But we had to find out what that meant, because one of us needs his own time a bit more than the other. Well, actually, significantly more than the other. So our challenge was to find a happy balance.

Mike

I've always enjoyed my "me time." It's my way of recharging my internal battery. It could entail anything from sitting quietly alone, to working out, taking a walk, playing golf, watching TV or a movie, playing video games, or just doing nothing. Whatever it is in that moment that I feel like I will enjoy the most, I do for myself. That's the key for me: it's about enjoying myself, by myself.

I've always believed that "time enjoyed is not time wasted." Whatever I choose to do at that moment is something I enjoy, and if I enjoy it, then it fills my soul and my spirit. Which to me is the entire purpose behind creating your own time. So I never tend to care whether Jana or someone else sees what I'm doing as wasting time, because whatever I'm doing, I'm doing it for me and my reasons. Not for anyone else's.

Just like everything in life and relationships, balance is key. Jana and I agree that we need time together and time apart. Frankly, it's healthy to miss each other. Which tends to be an issue with us at times because we work, live, and usually play together. So to keep a balance, sometimes we have to actively separate a bit. Having said that, I know that there is a hierarchy here. Sometimes we have busy weeks or days, and both time alone and time together can't be squeezed in. But if we have to choose between time together and time alone, we choose together. We never want our individual needs to come before the needs of our coupledom.

Jana

I'm just gonna hop right in and say I have such a hard time with this one. So much so that I was like, Meh, does this even have to be part of this chapter? The truth is I LOVE to spend time with Mike. I would rather spend all day with him than have my own time. It's not even that we have to be doing things together; I'm fine with just vegging on the couch together, to be in his presence and share experiences together.

I probably sound like an obsessive teenager, but that's how I've always been. I love being around people. I would rather stay at a friend's house than a hotel, rather talk to the stranger next to me on an airplane than be quiet. Fun fact: I even met one of my best friends doing that. You just never know who you're going to meet on your adventure of life.

Needless to say, the social distancing and shelter in place happening at the time of this book's publication because of the coronavirus did not help me in this area. I'm basically the Oprah of hugs—"You get a hug, you get a hug, and YOU get a hug!" So not being able to have that consistent connection with those closest to me outside of my husband was truly a struggle.

But back to my husband. He LOVES his alone time. I mean so much so that he would be totally fine with spending the entire day without me, and I truly think his idea of a great day would be seeing movies by himself followed by lounging solo. I used to have a problem with this because it felt super personal—like, *You don't want to hang out with me?*

What I've learned, though, is that it's not about me. It's about what he needs for his happiness. Contrary to the things I just said, I do like my own time, too. I like to sit outside in our screened-in porch, drink my wine, and escape the noise of the day in peace. I also love to go for hikes, and I feel rejuvenated with a healthy mind when I have that time. But I'm good with that for only about thirty minutes, and then I want my partner in crime back by my side.

At the end of the day, having your own time is a healthy thing. Not only can it make you miss your partner, but it can also help you feel more united. Your partner might have missed having you around, or maybe wanted you to experience what he just went through. It also helps with maybe making her appreciate you more, which I know is a huge one for husbands. Ladies, back away from your man every now and again. I promise that those men are going to appreciate you a hell of a lot more and vice versa. It's also good to have your own identity through outside activities. If your partner wants to golf and you have no interest in golfing (we obviously know who loves golf in our situation), it's a way for your partner to go out and enjoy what he loves to do, which in turn will have him returning to you refreshed and recharged.

Having your own time can also be a necessity so that you can be a better version of yourself, and who can fault you for that? The important thing is to be cautious of how much time you spend alone or together. You don't want to have so much intentional time together that you start to resent your partner because you're missing out on activities you want to be doing alone. Having healthy boundaries and open communication about them will help you both get what you want and need.

JANA'S ALONE TIME	MIKE'S ALONE TIME
Taking a long shower	Going to a movie solo
Going for a walk or working out	Golfing
Counting the hours till Mike wants to hang with me again :)	Playing video games
Sitting in my screened-in porch drinking wine	Doing anything in the garage

We want y'all to leave this chapter motivated to live your lives with more, you guessed it, INTENTION! Dilute some of those daily distractions. Instead of scrolling through Instagram posts during your lunch break, read an article on something you're interested in. Or listen to a favorite podcast. (We won't judge you if you wanna tune in to the latest episode of *Whine Down with Jana Kramer and Mike Caussin*.) Those small moments we have throughout our days are opportunities to do something with more purpose, more intention.

It can all come back full circle in your relationship, too. Instead of coming home to your loved one and saying, "OMG, did you see that post so-and-so put up?," you could be coming home and sharing that you just read this amazing article about [fill in the blank]. That could spark a more significant and soul-satisfying conversation between you and your partner, rather than just gossipy catch-up. No one feels better after gossiping, but most do after having a discussion around a passion or interest. By being intentional with just fifteen minutes of your day, you not only feed your soul with healthy material, you also create an opportunity for you and your partner to learn something about each other.

And while we're on the topic of learning about each other, we figure this is a good time to look at love languages.

Love Languages

Love languages have been widely talked about since Gary Chapman published his book *The Five Love Languages* in 1992. Funny thing is, though, not many people know their love languages, and even fewer know those of their spouse. You may nod when someone brings it up, but have you actually taken the test to determine your love languages? If not, you might not be loving your partner the way he or she can receive it. For us, learning each other's love languages was the start of a deeper understanding between us. At the end of the day, we all want to feel loved, so don't you want to know how to love your partner the best way you possibly can?

Chapman identifies five love languages, or ways we show love for another person and experience love:

1. Through words of affirmation

2. Through quality time

3. Through acts of service

4. Through physical touch

5. Through gift giving

Though most people value all five love languages to a degree, it's important to identify the top one or two that affect you the most. Jana's top two are physical touch and quality time; Michael's are acts of service and words of affirmation. You can see that the way we experience and show love—our love languages—aren't similar at all.

A common miss in relationships has to do with love languages, because it's natural for a person to show love in the way that he or she likes to receive it. For most of us we probably feel that our way is the correct way to show, express, or receive love because we've never known anything different. It may also be difficult to show or express love differently because you may not agree with or understand how your partner's top love language can be something that seems so foreign to you. But if you show up for your partner and love that person using the love language she or he understands, you'll be showing a deeper appreciation for your loved one. You're showing that you're willing to make that extra effort.

Jana

I'll never forget the first day I learned how Mike receives love. It was after a romantic night and a forty-five-minute massage. At the end of the night, he noticed that I had cleaned out my trash from his car. I'm the WORST for leaving empty water bottles, gum wrappers, and just basically making any car my burial ground. He came in the door beaming. When he told me how much that meant to him, I gave him one of those looks like, What the F are you talking about? He honestly was more excited about my picking up my gum wrappers from his car than the forty-five-minute massage I had just given him.

This was the most shocking thing to me in the world because what I would give for a massage from him! And that's when it clicked. As much as he loved the massage, that's just not the way Mike registers love. The fact that I had picked up my junk from his car and thrown it away showed him more love than anything else I could have done. That's when I learned that acts of service tops Michael's list of love languages.

Now here's the kicker: my ultimate number one love language, physical touch, is toward the bottom of his list. Michael could do all the dishes in the world, he could clean my car ten million times over, he could buy me hundreds of gifts . . . which are all very nice and sweet things and I'll always be nice and say "thank you." But those things aren't what make my heart skip a beat. Those things aren't what show me that he loves me. But if he comes up to me in the kitchen and wraps his arms around me—*that* makes my heart skip a beat. That's the biggest way he can say he loves me, through physical touch.

Let's go deeper into this. Have you ever been in an argument with your husband, and he comes home with flowers in hand expecting forgiveness? When you see the flowers, what do you feel? Would you categorize those feelings as happy/grateful or angry/resentful? Think about a scenario just like or similar to this and reflect on how you felt. If you were happy and receptive, then amazing, gifts may be one of your love languages. But if gifts don't do it for you, you might have responded with more of a "What the fuck, does he think flowers are really gonna fix this?!"

Knowing your spouse's love language is key when it comes to communication—or better yet, when repairing after a fight. You can use that knowledge to your advantage. For instance, after we fight, we try to speak with the other's love languages in order to repair more quickly. Jana may clean up the house a bit more or make the bed because she knows that acts of service is Mike's number one love language. And Mike might give Jana a few more hugs or simple touches throughout the day to speak to physical touch.

Of course, learning your love language isn't about just understanding your partner; it's also about doing some introspective work on yourself and knowing more about you. Of course, it's possible to identify with all five of the love languages because who wouldn't want a gift, or a spouse to do the dishes, or to be told nice things, or to be held or spend quality time with the person you love? The difference is identifying which one (or two) really makes your heart skip a beat—like Jana talked about. Which one makes you say, "Wow, he/she really loves me."

It's important to note that love languages aren't just a good tool for you and your partner. They can also be valuable assets to help you with any relationship in your life—best friend, sibling, parent, or anyone you have a close relationship with. Maybe your mom values words of affirmation and she needs you just to call her up and say "I love you," or maybe it's gifts so you send her flowers. Identifying a person's top love language can help you express your affection in the most powerful way.

We hope you're able to leave this chapter with a little bit more insight on how being intentional in your relationship and understanding your partner's love languages can be vital in showing your partner that you choose him or her. Don't shy away from discussing what those look like in your relationship, because they are different for everybody. In addition, make sure to bring up what you need for yourself in your relationship in order to be the best partner you can be. Happy connecting!

11 Trust the Process

Jana

After coming in fourth place on *Dancing with the Stars* I went straight to Michigan to celebrate Thanksgiving with my family. Mike and Jolie went with me, but if you had told me he wasn't there, I would have believed you. The atmosphere between us was quiet and cold, and frankly, it was awkward for everybody. I knew I had to make a decision about our marriage. My stalling over the previous three months while I was on the show had come to an end, and it was back to Nashville to figure out who was staying in the house and who was leaving.

Our therapist walked in to revisit where we had left off the days before Mike checked into rehab, and there we were sitting five feet apart on a couch. In my mind, I didn't see a way we could possibly reconcile, so the only option was to divorce. As soon as I muttered those words, our therapist stopped me. She said, "No major life changes for a year." To which I replied, "Are you kidding?" She went on to say that in her experience, it's best to not make any huge life decisions for a year after a traumatic event so you have time to process all the information and to cool down. I sat there dumbfounded, blinking at her with an empty feeling in my soul. Then I said, "How in the actual fuck am I supposed to stay in this relationship for another year? There is NO way!"

Making Up

Obviously, we had to start somewhere, and that just came down to a whole lot of making up. Which, as we all know, can be much more easily said than done. We've all been in that place where there's no light at the end of the tunnel and we wonder how in the world we're going to crawl out of this one. That was us on a regular basis early on. Take a second to reimagine that time when you're in the "making-up process" after an argument. Do you feel those anxious and frustrating feelings coming back up? Now, imagine dealing with that shit damn near every single day. Yup, you guessed it—it sucked.

As much as it sucked, we understood that in our situation it was going to be a process on a grand scale. Eventually, we found that light which for us was reconciliation. But even after that, it's not like the art of making up goes away. It had only just begun. In our experience, making up involves some of the things we've looked at in previous chapters, such as apologizing, cleaning your side of the street, and forgiving. But even when you pay attention to and make an effort to do all those things, making up still can be hard.

So how do we do it? Well, we don't do it perfectly each time, of course, but one way is to go do something fun together. It's all about reenergizing after some time away—maybe with something simple, like doing something as a family or watching a movie together. It's about igniting a new spark. We've all been on the tail end of an argument, and the other person extends an olive branch to go do something together. Even though we might not want to, we do a good job at trying. The end result is typically the same: we usually come back more connected. It's our way of jump-starting the battery and thrusting ourselves into a situation that makes us get out of our own way. Sometimes it's hard to get out of the emotions, but doing it for the good of the relationship, to try to restart it, is worth it, we promise. Just remember, you have to be willing to meet your partner halfway; because like most things, it takes the two of you to be successful.

Stay Present

Not to sound redundant, but this whole making-up process is easier said than done. And here's the deal: the only way we can make up is by focusing on just the topic or issue at hand. We have to stay present in the moment. If we start bringing up past shit, then we aren't going to move on from anything. Or if one of us starts playing the "what-if" game, then that just sets us up for failure in the future. We try our best not to make it about anything except the particular scenario in the present.

Jana

Be present. These are the hardest words for me to live by. The first year after I discovered Mike's infidelities, I kept bringing up the past and asking questions like, "Didn't our marriage or the birth of our baby girl mean anything to you?" I was constantly trying to understand everything and have it make "sense" to me. The problem is, going to the past is never going to help you make sense of the present. At least in my case it didn't.

After going to the past, then it was future tripping. I would worry about what he was "probably" going to do if he went to a bar or if he met someone. Or I would think about how my life was going to explode if he stepped out again on his family and relapsed.

Both of these ways of living and questioning were toxic to our relationship, for sure, but extremely toxic for me and my well-being. I would often sit with my therapist and ask her how I was going to stop having these thoughts, and she "simply" told me to stop ruminating (see the sidebar). It's so easy to be consumed by the pain and hurt of the past, but living in it day by day and replaying old thoughts and images just isn't going to do anything for you. I say that to remind myself because it's very easy to go down memory lane or what-if land.

It's not like I welcome those triggers in my life. Sometimes, they come out of nowhere, even if Mike and I are good. I can be watching a movie that takes me right back to questioning or thinking about the past. Or I can be driving down a street where I know some things went down. The second I start thinking about it, there comes the pain. It takes every ounce of my being to stay in the moment and be present. It's truly the best thing you can do for you and your relationship. In all honesty that's why we left Nashville for two years and moved to LA. We needed a place that didn't have physical triggers of the past so we could try to heal and repair. And before we moved back to Nashville we had to do the work on those certain landmarks so that we wouldn't spiral out of control when we returned from LA. But if I told you I didn't go to a certain hotel and cry my eyes out in the car knowing what went down three years prior when we moved back to Nashville, well, I would be lying. But here is what works for me, and obviously I don't do it right every time, but many times when I start to go down the rabbit hole of thoughts, I repeat to myself, "Stay present, stay present." I remind myself that I am in TODAY. Not tomorrow, not a week from now, not four years ago. *Today* my husband is being faithful. *Today* we are good. *Today* we are united.

What Is Rumination?

Rumination is continuously thinking the same thoughts over and over. The thoughts tend to be sad or dark. Ruminating can be isolating and can prolong or intensify anxiety and depression. It can be very hard to get out of that cycle when it starts. Here are some tips we've used to try to stay present when rumination comes up:

- Go for a walk
- Distract yourself by coloring, reading a book, or playing a game

- Call a friend
- Meditate

It's also important to speak your thoughts, so talking with a therapist to help your mind become unstuck is healthy and worth your time and money.

Mike

When Jana and I hear the words "be present," we naturally relate them to the affairs I had. But for me, it looks a little different. As the "perpetrator" in this situation, it would be easy for me to "live in the present" because that sounds like a great deal for me—kind of like an emotional "get out of jail free card." So you're saying let's focus on right now and not on all the terrible things I did in the past? Awesome! I'm in! Where do I sign? And part of me felt that way in the beginning. I would say to Jana, "Come on babe, focus on the now; I'm not doing any of those things today. Why can't you see that?" That didn't help either of us.

Here's the difference for me. It's helpful and important to stay in the present when it comes to dealing with my shame about the past. Paying attention to the present keeps me in a healthy mindset focused on recovery. Where I misconstrued staying in the present was when it came to Jana's pain and my empathy for it. When I said things like "I'm not doing that today," she saw me showing zero empathy for her pain. So my staying in the present that way didn't benefit either of us and caused more damage to our relationship in those moments.

In our marriage we've had to find that perfect balance between processing the past, seizing the present, and preparing for the future. We have benefited from keeping our focus on making the most of today by controlling what we can control in each moment. There are an infinite number of quotations and thoughts from very smart people around the world regarding staying present. I'll leave you with the one from my twelve-step meetings that has really stayed with me: "If you have one foot in yesterday and one foot in tomorrow, then you are in the perfect position to shit on today."

Piece by Piece

After we've been so vulnerable throughout this book and have let you in on some of our darkest times, you might be wondering, "How the fuck did they stay in that relationship?" We ultimately decided that it wasn't the end of the world for us, even though it felt like it at times. It took a while to realize that because early and often, every fight felt like the "this is over" fight. Later on, we would shake our heads and sometimes even laugh at how we handled some of our arguments and past triggers. At the time those arguments, fears, and worries seemed larger than life and almost too much to handle or bear. But ultimately we learned to "trust the process"—words we heard so often from therapists and even from people who were struggling with the same fight we were experiencing. It always seems easier said than done; but like anything, it's a process, and some days may just be harder than others. We didn't hit the ground running and immediately take to the concept of "trusting the process." It started by slowly piecing everything together, one piece at a time.

If you're in the middle of an explosion now, we see you and have so much empathy for that fragile place. We completely get it and see how everything might seem impossible to you. But after every big explosion, the dust eventually starts to settle, the air starts to clear. But it takes time. It also takes grace, and it takes a whole ton of empathy. What we've seen with our Good Fight is that it's truly a time game, which is hard for those of us who are impatient. No one wants to sit in pain, so you might look for a way to feel better faster, but that doesn't always lead to the best outcome. It takes time, and all the steps we've looked at in the previous chapters, to start seeing the outcome that you want. It's about trusting the steps, trusting your decision, and sometimes just trusting your gut to stay and fight The Good Fight.

Speaking of The Good Fight, we came up with this acronym during the process of writing this book. It will help you remember five of the most necessary tools you need to turn your relationship fight into The Good Fight.

The Good Fight

F—Forgiveness

I—Intention

G—Grace

H—Humility

T—Trust

First, you need to *forgive*. And in order to fight The Good Fight, you need to have *intention* with your time, your words, and how you love. You need to have *grace* for yourself, for your partner, for the journey you're on, and for the moments when shit hits the fan. You need to have *humility*—to be able to lean in, own your mistakes, say you're sorry, and ask for what you need. Finally, *trust* comes when you're in The Good Fight.

Silver Lining in Repair

Every relationship has its shit, and there is not a universal scale that measures the magnitude of a person's feelings. Feelings in a relationship and in life are all subjective. So we can never say that one person's feelings or pain in a situation is greater than someone else's in a different scenario—or even in the same scenario. It's all specific to that individual and their experience.

We chose to stay married and fight The Good Fight. That was our choice, and nothing we have been through can be categorized as greater than anyone else's experiences in their relationships. But we will say that as we have trudged through all of our trauma, triggers, pain, and sadness these past few years, we have truly started to see that light at the end of the tunnel—what we like to call the silver lining in repair.

The reconciliation process in a relationship is typically not easy. We found ourselves constantly wondering whether the darkness was ever going to end. But not only are our darkest days behind us; we have come out of them better people. So even if the worst-case scenario happens and we don't finish our lives together as a couple, then at least we came out the other side better than we were going in. We think it's important to emphasize that for a minute: because of the shit we've been through, and our hard work and dedication, we have become and are continuing to become better individuals. This journey has not been solely for us as a couple or for Jolie and Jace. It ultimately has been for ourselves as individuals, because you can't change who you are or parts about yourself for the better if you're only motivated by doing it for someone or something else.

It's safe to say that five years ago on our picture-perfect wedding day we never could have imagined being in this situation—let alone writing a book about the heartbreak, the loss, the lies, and the failure. But we've also been writing about hope, strength, commitment, growth, and LOVE. Four years ago we were on our knees and in the darkest time of our lives. We never could have imagined that going through that hell we ultimately would find our silver lining in repair.

We understand that it may be hard to see that silver lining. We understand that you might not have all the answers. Lord knows, we didn't, and we still don't to this day. We still don't know the outcome, and though we are hopeful, we have to continue to actively fight together—to fight The Good Fight—to make our relationship the best it can be. We need to keep using the tools and to continue to grow together.

Since discovery, we've been hurt beyond belief, but not beyond repair. We truly believe that no matter how shattered or broken two people might be, if they are willing to show up and do the work, there is hope for repair. It's not easy, and by no means will our journey always be perfect and effortless, but we're in the ring together. Sometimes, that isn't the answer, and it's just not meant to be. But at the end of the day, we're willing to do this together with the love we have for each other. We will always show up for The Good Fight.

Wherever you are in your journey right now, whether you're broken, confused, or just simply wanting to grow and garner more tools, just remember that you're not alone. We are cheering you on from the sidelines. So if you're willing to grow for yourself and for your partner, give it a try. Commit to the work, commit to the process, and find your silver lining in repair. You are strong enough, you are good enough, and you are not alone. So no more sitting on the sidelines. Go earn the life and love you deserve!

> *I did then what I knew how to do.*
> *Now that I know better, I do better.*
>
> —MAYA ANGELOU

Acknowledgments

We first and foremost thank our friends and family, who through these past years of trials, tribulations, pain, and growth have remained unwaveringly supportive. To our parents, neither one of us would have the strength, stamina, resolve, or grace of forgiveness if it weren't for the values you have instilled in us throughout our lives. A giant thank-you to all of our couples' and individual therapists over the years: Dan Drake, Bill and Laurie Lokey, Aaron Alan, Marc Pimsler, and Amy Alexander. There is no way we would be even close to where we are today if it weren't for your commitment to us as individuals and as a couple. Of all people in our lives you knew every dark secret of every dark corner, and you still did not give up on us—for that we are eternally grateful. To our amazingly talented and devoted editor Sydney Rogers (and the rest of the HarperOne team) as well as our agent Margaret King Riley; thank you both for breathing life into this project and motivating us to turn it into what it has become. We could not have done this without you. Last, we acknowledge that it is primarily due to God's will that this book has become a reality. It is because of Him that we still stand hand in hand as husband and wife. He has mended our hearts and is driving our story forward as we continue on this beautiful journey called life.

Resources

Here are some websites, books, and programs that have helped us. Maybe they can provide a starting place for you to find some help and support, too.

Love & Respect (website), https://www.loveandrespect.com/, and Emerson Eggerichs, *Love & Respect: The Love She Most Desires; the Respect He Desperately Needs* (Nashville: Thomas Nelson, 2004).

The 5 Love Languages (website), https://www.5lovelanguages .com/, and Gary Chapman, *The 5 Love Languages: The Secret to Love That Lasts* (1992; Chicago: Northfield, 2015).

Stephen M. Arterburn and Jason B. Martinkus, *Worthy of Her Trust: What You Need to Do to Rebuild Sexual Integrity and Win Her Back* (Colorado Springs: WaterBrook, 2014).

Don Miguel Ruiz, *The Four Agreements: A Practical Guide to Personal Freedom* (San Rafael, CA: Amber-Allen, 1997).

SAA (Sex Addicts Anonymous) (website), https://saa-recovery.org: "A fellowship of men and women who share their experience, strength and hope with each other so they may overcome their sexual addiction and help others recover from sexual addiction or dependency."

Onsite, center for personal growth and emotional wellness (website), https://www.onsiteworkshops.com/our-beliefs/.